MW00845681

Python for Secret Agents

Analyze, encrypt, and uncover intelligence data using Python, the essential tool for all aspiring secret agents

Steven F. Lott

[PACKT] open source ✳
PUBLISHING   community experience distilled

BIRMINGHAM - MUMBAI

Python for Secret Agents

Copyright © 2014 Packt Publishing

All rights reserved. No part of this book may be reproduced, stored in a retrieval system, or transmitted in any form or by any means, without the prior written permission of the publisher, except in the case of brief quotations embedded in critical articles or reviews.

Every effort has been made in the preparation of this book to ensure the accuracy of the information presented. However, the information contained in this book is sold without warranty, either express or implied. Neither the author, nor Packt Publishing, and its dealers and distributors will be held liable for any damages caused or alleged to be caused directly or indirectly by this book.

Packt Publishing has endeavored to provide trademark information about all of the companies and products mentioned in this book by the appropriate use of capitals. However, Packt Publishing cannot guarantee the accuracy of this information.

First published: August 2014

Production reference: 1190814

Published by Packt Publishing Ltd.
Livery Place
35 Livery Street
Birmingham B3 2PB, UK.

ISBN 978-1-78398-042-0

www.packtpub.com

Cover image by Jarek Blaminsky (milak6@wp.pl)

Credits

Author
Steven F. Lott

Reviewers
Nick Glynn
Steven Heinrich
Sanjeev Jaiswal
Maurice HT Ling

Acquisition Editor
Sam Wood

Content Development Editor
Prachi Bisht

Technical Editors
Veena Pagare
Anand Singh

Copy Editors
Insiya Morbiwala
Sayanee Mukherjee
Deepa Nambiar
Karuna Narayanan
Adithi Shetty
Laxmi Subramanian

Project Coordinator
Sageer Parkar

Proofreaders
Ameesha Green
Samantha Lyon

Indexers
Hemangini Bari
Rekha Nair

Graphics
Sheetal Aute

Production Coordinator
Nilesh R. Mohite

Cover Work
Nilesh R. Mohite

About the Author

Steven F. Lott has been programming since the 70s, when computers were large, expensive, and rare. As a contract software developer and architect, he has worked on hundreds of projects, from very small to very large ones. He's been using Python to solve business problems for over 10 years.

He's particularly adept in struggling with gnarly data representation problems. He is also the author of *Mastering Object-oriented Python*, *Packt Publishing*.

He is currently a technomad who lives in various places on the East Coast of the U.S. His technology blog is located at `http://slott-softwarearchitect.blogspot.com`.

About the Reviewers

Nick Glynn is currently employed as a technical trainer and consultant delivering courses and expertise on Android, Python, and Linux at home in the UK and across the globe. He has a broad range of experience, from board bring-up, Linux driver development, and systems development to full stack deployments, web app development, and security hardening for both the Linux and Android platforms.

> I would like to thank my family for their love and my beautiful baby girl, Inara, for always brightening my day.

Steven Heinrich is a full stack web developer who specializes in geospatial applications. He has a Bachelor's degree in Geographic Information Systems (GIS) and a Master's degree in GIS Management, both from Salisbury University. Steve likes to stay updated on new technologies and build a diverse portfolio.

Working on a wide array of projects allows him to work with a tech stack that best fits the unique needs of each project. This versatility and his desire to learn new technologies keeps Steve energized and motivated.

Besides enjoying spending time with his family, sports, and being a tech geek, he relaxes by sipping on one of the many homebrewed beers on tap in his garage.

Sanjeev Jaiswal is a computer graduate with 5 years of industrial experience. He basically uses Perl and GNU/Linux for his day-to-day work. He also teaches Drupal and WordPress CMS to bloggers. He has worked closely with top companies such as CSC, IBM, and Motorola Mobility. He has also developed an interest in web application penetration testing since 2013.

Sanjeev loves to impart his technical knowledge to engineering students and IT professionals and has been teaching since 2008. He founded Alien Coders (`http://www.aliencoders.com/`) based on the *learning through sharing* principle for computer science students and IT professionals in 2010 and has become a huge hit in India among engineering students.

He usually uploads technical videos on YouTube under the `Alien Coders` tag. He has a huge fan base on his site because of his simple yet effective way of teaching and his philanthropic nature towards students. You can follow him at `http://www.facebook.com/aliencoders` on Facebook and `http://twitter.com/aliencoders` on Twitter.

He has authored *Instant PageSpeed Optimization*, *Packt Publishing*, and is looking forward to author or review more books by Packt Publishing and other publishers.

I would like to thank my parents and my wife, Shalini Jaiswal, for their moral support in every phase of my life and growth.

I also give deep thanks and gratitude to my best friends, Ritesh Kamal and Ranjan Pandey, for their personal and professional help that is always available. It is because of them and some of my best friends, Rakesh Pandey, Rakesh Sharma, Abhishek Shukla, Anil Sharma, Santosh Vishwakarma, and others, that I have achieved a set of impossible goals in such a short time.

Maurice HT Ling (personal website: `http://maurice.vodien.com`) has completed his PhD in Bioinformatics and BSc (Hons) in Molecular and Cell Biology from The University of Melbourne. He is currently a research fellow at Nanyang Technological University, Singapore, and an honorary fellow at The University of Melbourne, Australia. Maurice is the chief editor of the journal, *Computational and Mathematical Biology, iConcept Press Ltd.*; the co-editor of the e-journal, *The Python Papers*; and the co-founder of the Python User Group (Singapore).

Recently, Maurice co-founded the first synthetic biology start-up in Singapore, AdvanceSyn Pte. Ltd., as Director and Chief Technology Officer. His research interests lie in life—biological life, artificial life, and artificial intelligence—using computer science and statistics as tools to understand life and its numerous aspects. In his free time, Maurice likes to read, enjoy a cup of coffee, write his personal journal, or philosophize on the various aspects of life.

www.PacktPub.com

Support files, eBooks, discount offers and more

You might want to visit www.PacktPub.com for support files and downloads related to your book.

Did you know that Packt offers eBook versions of every book published, with PDF and ePub files available? You can upgrade to the eBook version at www.PacktPub.com and as a print book customer, you are entitled to a discount on the eBook copy. Get in touch with us at service@packtpub.com for more details.

At www.PacktPub.com, you can also read a collection of free technical articles, sign up for a range of free newsletters and receive exclusive discounts and offers on Packt books and eBooks.

http://PacktLib.PacktPub.com

Do you need instant solutions to your IT questions? PacktLib is Packt's online digital book library. Here, you can access, read and search across Packt's entire library of books.

Why Subscribe?

- Fully searchable across every book published by Packt
- Copy and paste, print and bookmark content
- On demand and accessible via web browser

Free Access for Packt account holders

If you have an account with Packt at www.PacktPub.com, you can use this to access PacktLib today and view nine entirely free books. Simply use your login credentials for immediate access.

Table of Contents

Preface

Every secret agent needs a good set of tools and gadgets. When an agent's missions involve gathering data, high-powered data processing is required. This book will provide you with the kinds of information processing tools that will help you gather, analyze, and communicate the data that the HQ demands.

Python allows agents to write simple scripts to gather data, perform sophisticated calculations, and produce useful results. Agents can also use Python to extract data from local files, HTTP web servers, and FTP file servers.

Python has numerous add-on packages. This book will explore just two: Pillow allows for sophisticated image conversion and manipulation, and BeautifulSoup allows an agent to extract data from HTML web pages. Agents with specific needs might have to explore the Python Natural Language Toolkit (NLTK), Numeric Python (NumPy), or even Scientific Python (SciPy).

What this book covers

Chapter 1, *Our Espionage Toolkit*, exposes the basics of installing and using Python. We'll write scripts to help agents work with foreign currency conversions and learn how an agent can recover a lost password from a ZIP archive.

Chapter 2, *Acquiring Intelligence Data*, shows how we can use Python to extract information from various kinds of file servers. Agents will learn how to work with different Internet protocols and use Representational State Transfer (REST) to interact with web services. This will include techniques to work with cyptocurrencies, such as bitcoins.

Chapter 3, *Encoding Secret Messages with Steganography*, shows how we can add the Pillow toolset to work with images. An agent with Pillow can create thumbnails and convert, crop, and enhance images. We'll also explore some steganography algorithms to bury our messages in an image file.

Chapter 4, Drops, Hideouts, Meetups, and Lairs, provides a closer look at geocoding and geolocation. This includes the use of web services to convert an address into a latitude and longitude. We'll also learn how to convert a latitude and longitude back into an address. We'll take a look at the haversine formula to get the correct distance between locations. We'll also look at some of the ways in which geographic locations can be represented for tidy storage and communication.

Chapter 5, A Spymaster's More Sensitive Analyses, shows how we can use Python for a basic data analysis. A good agent doesn't just spout facts and figures; a good agent does enough analysis to confirm that the data is realistic. Being able to examine the correlation between datasets is what creates a valuable intelligence asset.

What you need for this book

A secret agent needs a computer that they have administrative privileges over. We'll be installing additional software. Without the administrative password, they may have trouble installing Python 3, Pillow, or BeautifulSoup.

For agents using Windows, the packages we're looking at adding come prebuilt.

For agents using Linux, the developer tools are required. Linux has a complete suite of developer tools that are common. The Gnu C Compiler (GCC) is the backbone of these tools.

For agents using Mac OS X, the developer tool, Xcode (`https://developer.apple.com/xcode/`), is required. We'll also need to install a tool called homebrew (`http://brew.sh`) to help us add the Linux packages to Mac OS X.

Python 3 is available from the Python download page at `https://www.python.org/download`.

We'll download and install several things besides Python 3.3:

- The setuptools package, which includes `easy_install-3.3`, will help us add packages. It can be downloaded from `https://pypi.python.org/pypi/setuptools`.

- The PIP package will also help us install additional packages. Some experienced field agents prefer PIP over setuptools. It can be downloaded from `https://pypi.python.org/pypi/pip/1.5.6`.

- The Pillow package will allow us to work with image files. It can be downloaded from `https://pypi.python.org/pypi/Pillow/2.4.0`.

- The BeautifulSoup Version 4 package will allow us to work with HTML web pages. It can be downloaded from `https://pypi.python.org/pypi/beautifulsoup4/4.3.2`.

From this, we'll see how extensible Python is. Almost anything an agent might need may already be written and available through the Python Package Index (PyPi), which can be downloaded from `https://pypi.python.org/pypi`.

Who this book is for

This book is for secret agents who don't know much Python, but are comfortable installing new software and are ready to do some clever programming in Python. An agent who has never done any programming before might find some of this a bit advanced; a beginner's tutorial that covers the basics of Python may be helpful.

We'll expect that an agent using this book is comfortable with simple math. This involves the multiplication and division of currency conversions. It also includes polynomials, simple trigonometry, and a few statistical formulae.

We also expect the secret agents using this book to be doing their own investigations. The book's examples are designed to get the agent started down the road with developing interesting, useful applications. Each agent will have to explore further afield on their own.

Conventions

In this book, you will find a number of styles of text that distinguish between different kinds of information. Here are some examples of these styles, and an explanation of their meaning.

Code words in text, package names, folder names, filenames, file extensions, pathnames, dummy URLs, user input, and Twitter handles are shown as follows: "The `size_list` variable is a sequence of eight-tuples built from the bytes of the encoded size."

A block of code is set as follows:

```
message_bytes= message.encode("UTF-8")
bits_list = list(to_bits(c) for c in message_bytes )
len_h, len_l = divmod( len(message_bytes), 256 )
size_list = [to_bits(len_h), to_bits(len_l)]
bit_sequence( size_list+bits_list )
```

When we wish to draw your attention to a particular part of a code block, the relevant lines or items are set in bold:

```
w, h = ship.size
for p,m in enumerate( bit_sequence(size_list+bits_list) ):
    y, x = divmod( p, w )
    r, g, b = ship.getpixel( (x,y) )
    r_new = (r & 0xfe) | m
    print( (r, g, b), m, (r_new, g, b) )
    ship.putpixel( (x,y), (r_new, g, b)  )
```

Any command-line input or output is written as follows:

```
$ python3.3 -m doctest ourfile.py
```

New terms and **important words** are shown in bold. Words that you see on the screen, in menus or dialog boxes for example, appear in the text like this: "There is an **Advanced Settings** panel that defines these file associations."

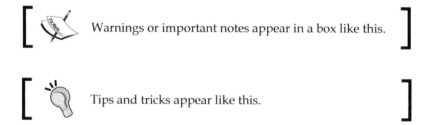

> Warnings or important notes appear in a box like this.

> Tips and tricks appear like this.

Reader feedback

Feedback from our readers is always welcome. Let us know what you think about this book—what you liked or may have disliked. Reader feedback is important for us to develop titles that you really get the most out of.

To send us general feedback, simply send an e-mail to `feedback@packtpub.com`, and mention the book title via the subject of your message.

If there is a topic that you have expertise in and you are interested in either writing or contributing to a book, see our author guide on `www.packtpub.com/authors`.

Customer support

Now that you are the proud owner of a Packt Publishing book, we have a number of things to help you to get the most from your purchase.

Downloading the example code

You can download the example code files for all Packt Publishing books you have purchased from your account at http://www.packtpub.com. If you purchased this book elsewhere, you can visit http://www.packtpub.com/support and register to have the files e-mailed directly to you.

Errata

Although we have taken every care to ensure the accuracy of our content, mistakes do happen. If you find a mistake in one of our books—maybe a mistake in the text or the code—we would be grateful if you would report this to us. By doing so, you can save other readers from frustration and help us improve subsequent versions of this book. If you find any errata, please report them by visiting http://www.packtpub.com/submit-errata, selecting your book, clicking on the **errata submission form** link, and entering the details of your errata. Once your errata are verified, your submission will be accepted and the errata will be uploaded on our website, or added to any list of existing errata, under the Errata section of that title. Any existing errata can be viewed by selecting your title from http://www.packtpub.com/support.

Piracy

Piracy of copyright material on the Internet is an ongoing problem across all media. At Packt Publishing, we take the protection of our copyright and licenses very seriously. If you come across any illegal copies of our works, in any form, on the Internet, please provide us with the location address or website name immediately so that we can pursue a remedy.

Please contact us at copyright@packtpub.com with a link to the suspected pirated material.

We appreciate your help in protecting our authors, and our ability to bring you valuable content.

Questions

You can contact us at questions@packtpub.com if you are having a problem with any aspect of the book, and we will do our best to address it.

1
Our Espionage Toolkit

The job of espionage is to gather and analyze data. This requires us to use computers and software tools.

The ordinary *desktop* tools (word processor, spreadsheet, and so on) will not measure up for the kinds of jobs we need to tackle. For serious data gathering, analysis, and dissemination, we need more powerful tools. As we look at automating our data gathering, we can't easily use a desktop tool that requires manual pointing and clicking. We want a tool that can be left to run autonomously working for us without anyone sitting at a desk.

One of the most powerful data analysis tools we can use is Python. We're going to step through a series of examples of real data collection and analysis using Python. This chapter will cover the following topics:

- Firstly, we're going to download and install the latest and greatest Python release.
- We're going to supplement Python with the `easy_install` (or `pip`) tools to help us gather additional software tools in the later chapters.
- We'll look at Python's internal help system briefly.
- We'll look at how Python works with numbers. After all, a secret agent's job of collecting data is going to involve numbers.
- We'll spend some time on the first steps of writing Python applications. We'll call our applications scripts as well as modules.
- We'll break file input and output into several sections. We will have a quick overview as well as an in-depth look at ZIP archive files. In the later chapters, we'll look at more kinds of files.
- Our big mission will be to apply our skills for recovering a lost password for a ZIP file. This won't be easy, but we should have covered enough of the basics to be successful.

This will give us enough Python skills so that we can advance to more complex missions in the next chapters.

Getting the tools of the trade – Python 3.3

The first step toward using Python is getting the Python language onto our computer. If your computer uses Mac OS X or Linux, you may already have Python available. At the time of this writing, it's Python 2.7, not 3.3. In this case, we will need to install Python 3.3 in addition to Python 2.7 we already have.

Windows agents generally don't have any version of Python, and need to install Python 3.3.

 Python 3 is not *Python 2.7 plus a few features*. Python 3 is a distinct language. We don't cover Python 2.7 in this book. The examples won't work in Python 2. Really.

Python downloads are available at `http://www.python.org/download/`.

Locate the proper version for your computer. There are many pre-built binaries for Windows, Linux, and Mac OS X. Linux agents should focus on the binary appropriate to their distribution. Each download and install will be a bit different; we can't cover all the details.

There are several implementations of Python. We'll focus on CPython. For some missions, you might want to look at Jython, which is Python implemented using the Java Virtual Machine. If you're working with other .NET products, you might need Iron Python. In some cases, you might be interested in PyPy, which is Python implemented in Python. (And, yes, it seems circular and contradictory. It's really interesting, but well outside our focus.)

Python isn't the only tool. It's the starting point. We'll be downloading additional tools in the later chapters. It seems like half of our job as a secret agent is locating the tools required to crack open a particularly complex problem. The other half is actually getting the information.

Windows secrets

Download the Windows installer for Python 3.3 (or higher) for your version of Windows. When you run the installer, you'll be asked a number of questions about where to install it and what to install.

It's essential that Python be installed in a directory with a simple name. Under Windows, the common choice is `C:\Python33`. Using the Windows directories with spaces in their name (`Program Files`, `My Documents`, or `Documents and Settings`) can cause confusion.

Be sure to install the Tcl/Tk components too. This will assure that you have all the elements required to support IDLE. **IDLE** is a handy text editor that comes with Python. For Windows agents, this is generally bundled into the installation kit. All you need to do is be sure it has a check mark in the installation wizard.

With Windows, the `python.exe` program doesn't have a version number as part of its name. This is atypical.

Mac OS X secrets

In Mac OS X, there is already a Python installation, usually Python 2.7. This must be left intact.

Download the Mac OS X installer for Python 3.3 (or higher). When you run this, you will be adding a second version of Python. This means that many add-on modules and tools must be associated with the proper version of Python. This requires a little bit of care. It's not good to use the vaguely-named tool like `easy_install`. It's important to use the more specific `easy_install-3.3`, which identifies the version of Python you're working with.

The program named `python` is usually going to be an alias for `python2.7`. This, too, must be left intact. We'll always explicitly use `python3` (also known as `python3.3`) for this book. You can confirm this by using the shell command.

Note that there are several versions of Tcl/Tk available for Mac OS X. The Python website directs you to a specific version. At the time of this writing, this version was ActiveTCL 8.5.14 from ActiveState software. You'll need to install this, too. This software allows us to use IDLE.

Visit `http://www.activestate.com/activetcl/downloads` for the proper version.

Getting more tools – a text editor

To create Python applications, we're going to need a proper programmers' text editor. A word processor won't do because the files created by a word processor are too complex. We need simple text. Our emphasis is on simplicity. Python3 works in Unicode without bolding or italicizing the content. (Python 2 didn't work as well with Unicode. This is one of the reasons to leave it behind.)

If you've worked with text editors or **integrated development environments (IDEs)**, you may already have a favorite. Feel free to use it. Some of the popular IDEs have Python support.

Python is called a dynamic language. It's not always simple to determine what names or keywords are legal in a given context. The Python compiler doesn't perform a lot of static checking. An IDE can't easily prompt with a short list of all legal alternatives. Some IDEs do take a stab at having logical suggestions, but they're not necessarily complete.

If you haven't worked with a programmer's editor (or an IDE), your first mission is to locate a text editor you can work with. Python includes an editor named IDLE that is easy to use. It's a good place to start.

The Active State Komodo Edit might be suitable (`http://komodoide.com/komodo-edit/`). It's a lightweight version of a commercial product. It's got some very clever ways to handle the dynamic language aspects of Python.

There are many other code editors. Your first training mission is to locate something you can work with. You're on your own. We have faith in you.

Getting other developer tools

Most GNU/Linux agents have various C compilers and other developer tools available. Many Linux distributions are already configured to support developers, so the tools are already there.

Mac OS X agents will usually need Xcode. Get it from `https://developer.apple.com/xcode/downloads/`. Every Mac OS X agent should have this.

When installing this, be sure to also install the command line developer tools. This is another big download above and beyond the basic Xcode download.

Windows agents will generally find that pre-built binaries are available for most packages of interest. If, in a rare case, that pre-built code isn't available, tools such as Cygwin may be necessary. See `http://www.cygwin.com`.

Getting a tool to get more Python components

In order to effectively and simply download additional Python modules, we often use a tool to get tools. There are two popular ways to add Python modules: PIP and the `easy_install` script.

To install `easy_install`, go to `https://pypi.python.org/pypi/setuptools/3.6`.

The `setuptools` package will include the `easy_install` script, which we'll use to add modules to Python.

If you've got multiple versions of Python installed, be sure to download and then install the correct easy install version for Python 3.3. This means that you'll generally be using the `easy_install-3.3` script to add new software tools.

To install PIP, go to `https://pypi.python.org/pypi/pip/1.5.6`.

We'll be adding the `Pillow` package in *Chapter 3, Encoding Secret Messages with Steganography*. We'll also be adding the `Beautiful Soup` package in *Chapter 4, Drops, Hideouts, Meetups, and Lairs*.

The Python 3.4 distribution should include the PIP tool. You don't need to download it separately.

Confirming our tools

To be sure we have a working Python tool, it's best to check things from the command prompt. We're going to do a lot of our work using the command prompt. It involves the least overhead and is the most direct connection to Python.

The Python 3.3 program shows a startup message that looks like this:

```
MacBookPro-SLott:Secret Agent's Python slott$ python3
Python 3.3.4 (v3.3.4:7ff62415e426, Feb  9 2014, 00:29:34)
[GCC 4.2.1 (Apple Inc. build 5666) (dot 3)] on darwin
Type help, copyright, credits or license for more information.
>>>
```

We've shown the operating system's prompt (`MacBookPro-SLott:Secret Agent's Python slott$`), the command we entered (`python3`), and the response from Python.

Python provides three lines of introduction followed by its own >>> prompt. The first line shows that it's Python 3.3.4. The second line shows the tools used to build Python (GCC 4.2.1). The third line provides some hints about things we might do next.

We've interacted with Python. Things are working.

Downloading the example code

You can download the example code files for all Packt books you have purchased from your account at `http://www.packtpub.com`. If you purchased this book elsewhere, you can visit `http://www.packtpub.com/support` and register to have the files e-mailed directly to you.

Feel free to enter `copyright`, `credits`, and `license` at the `>>>` prompt. They may be boring, but they serve as confirmation that things are working.

It's important to note that these objects (`copyright`, `credits`, and `license`) are not commands or verbs in the Python language. They're global variables that were created as a convenience for first-time Python agents. When evaluated, they display blocks of text.

There are two other startup objects we'll use: `exit` and `help`. These provide little messages that remind us to use the `help()` and `exit()` functions.

How do we stop?

We can always enter `exit` to get a reminder on how to exit from interactive Python, as follows:

```
>>> exit
```

Use `exit()` or *Ctrl* + *D* (that is **EOF (end-of-file)**) to exit.

Windows agents will see that they must use *Ctrl* + *Z* and `Return` to exit.

Python is a programming language that also has an interactive prompt of `>>>`. To confirm that Python is working, we're responding to that prompt, using a feature called the **Read-Execute-Print Loop (REPL)**.

In the long run, we'll be writing scripts to process our data. Our data might be an image or a secret message. The end of a script file will exit from Python. This is the same as pressing *Ctrl* + *D* (or *Ctrl* + *Z* and `Return`) to send the EOF sequence.

Using the help() system

Python has a help mode, which is started with the `help()` function. The `help()` function provides help on a specific topic. Almost anything you see in Python can be the subject of help.

For pieces of Python syntax, such as the + operator, you'll need to use a string meaning you should enclose the syntax in quotes. For example, `help("+")` will provide detailed help on operator precedence.

For other objects (such as numbers, strings, functions, classes, and modules) you can simply ask for help on the object itself; quotes aren't used. Python will locate the class of the object and provide help on the class.

For example, `help(3)` will provide a lot of detailed, technical help on integers, as shown in the following snippet:

```
>>> help(3)
Help on int object:
class int(object)
 |  int(x=0) -> integer
 |  int(x, base=10) -> integer
 |
etc.
```

When using the `help()` module from the command line, the output will be presented in pages. At the end of the first page of output, we see a new kind of non-Python prompt. This is usually `:`, but on Windows it may be `-- More --`.

Python normally prompts us with `>>>` or `....`. A non-Python prompt must come from one of the help viewers.

Mac OS and GNU/Linux secrets

In POSIX-compatible OSes, we'll be interacting with a program named `less`; it will prompt with `:` for all but the last page of your document. For the last page, it will prompt with `(END)`.

This program is very sophisticated; you can read more about it on Wikipedia at `http://en.wikipedia.org/wiki/Less_(Unix)`.

The four most important commands are as follows:

* `q`: This command is used to quit the `less` help viewer
* `h`: This command is used to get help on all the commands that are available
* `⌴`: This command is used to enter a space to see the next page
* `b`: This command is used to go back one page

Windows secrets

In Windows, we'll usually interact with a program named `more`; it will prompt you with `-- More --`. You can read more about it on Wikipedia from `http://en.wikipedia.org/wiki/More_(command)`.

The three important commands here are: `q`, `h`, and `⌴`.

Using the help mode

When we enter `help()` with no object or string value, we wind up in help mode. This uses Python's `help>` prompt to make it very clear that we're getting help, not entering Python statements. To go back to ordinary Python programming mode, and enter `quit`.

The prompt then changes back to `>>>` to confirm that we can go back to entering code.

Your next training mission is to experiment with the `help()` function and help mode before we can move on.

Background briefing – math and numbers

We'll review basics of Python programming before we start any of our more serious missions. If you already know a little Python, this should be a review. If you don't know any Python, this is just an overview and many details will be omitted.

If you've never done any programming before, this briefing may be a bit too brief. You might want to get a more in-depth tutorial. If you're completely new to programming, you might want to look over this page for additional tutorials: `https://wiki.python.org/moin/BeginnersGuide/NonProgrammers`. For more help to start with expert Python programming, go to `http://www.packtpub.com/expert-python-programming/book`.

The usual culprits

Python provides the usual mix of arithmetic and comparison operators. However, there are some important wrinkles and features. Rather than assuming you're aware of them, we'll review the details.

The conventional arithmetic operators are: `+`, `-`, `*`, `/`, `//`, `%`, and `**`. There are two variations on division: an exact division (`/`) and an integer division (`//`). You must choose whether you want an exact, floating-point result, or an integer result:

```
>>> 355/113
3.1415929203539825
>>> 355//113
3
>>> 355.0/113.0
3.1415929203539825
>>> 355.0//113.0
3.0
```

The exact division (/) produces a `float` result from two integers. The integer division produces an integer result. When we use `float` values, we expect exact division to produce `float`. Even with two floating-point values, the integer division produces a rounded-down floating-point result.

We have this extra division operator to avoid having to use wordy constructs such as `int(a/b)` or `math.floor(a/b)`.

Beyond conventional arithmetic, there are some additional **bit fiddling** operators that are available: `&`, `|`, `^`, `>>`, `<<`, and `~`. These operators work on integers (and sets). These are emphatically not Boolean operators; they don't work on the narrow domain of `True` and `False`. They work on the individual bits of an integer.

We'll use binary values with the `0b` prefix to show what the operators do, as shown in the following code. We'll look at details of this `0b` prefix later.

```
>>> bin(0b0101 & 0b0110)
'0b100'
>>> bin(0b0101 ^ 0b0110)
'0b11'
>>> bin(0b0101 | 0b0110)
'0b111'
>>> bin(~0b0101)
'-0b110'
```

The `&` operator does bitwise AND. The `^` operator does bitwise exclusive OR (XOR). The `|` operator does inclusive OR. The `~` operator is the complement of the bits. The result has many 1 bits and is shown as a negative number.

The `<<` and `>>` operators are for doing left and right shifts of the bits, as shown in the following code:

```
>>> bin( 0b110 << 4 )
'0b1100000'
>>> bin( 0b1100000 >> 3 )
'0b1100'
```

It may not be obvious, but shifting left x bits is like multiplying it by `2**x`, except it may operate faster. Similarly, shifting right by b bits amounts to division by `2**b`.

We also have all of the usual comparison operators: `<`, `<=`, `>`, `>=`, `==`, and `!=`.

In Python, we can combine comparison operators without including the AND operator:

```
>>> 7 <= 11 < 17
True
>>> 7 <= 11 and 11 < 17
True
```

This simplification really does implement our conventional mathematical understanding of how comparisons can be written. We don't need to say `7 <= 11 and 11 < 17`.

There's another comparison operator that's used in some specialized situations: `is`. The `is` operator will appear, for now, to be the same as `==`. Try it. `3 is 3` and `3 == 3` seem to do the same thing. Later, when we start using the `None` object, we'll see the most common use for the `is` operator. For more advanced Python programming, there's a need to distinguish between two references to the same object (`is`) and two objects which claim to have the same value (`==`).

The ivory tower of numbers

Python gives us a variety of numbers, plus the ability to easily add new kinds of numbers. We'll focus on the built-in numbers here. Adding new kinds of numbers is the sort of thing that takes up whole chapters in more advanced books.

Python ranks the numbers into a kind of tower. At the top are numbers with fewest features. Each subclass extends that number with more and more features. We'll look at the tower from bottom up, starting with the integers that have the most features, and moving towards the complex numbers that have the least features. The following sections cover the various kinds of numbers we'll need to use.

Integer numbers

We can write integer values in base 10, 16, 8, or 2. Base 10 numbers don't need a prefix, the other bases will use a simple two-character prefix, as shown in the following snippet:

```
48813
0xbead
0b1011111010101101
0o137255
```

We also have functions that will convert numbers into handy strings in different bases. We can use the `hex()`, `oct()`, and `bin()` functions to see a value in base 16, 8, or 2.

The question of integer size is common. Python integers don't have a maximum size. They're not artificially limited to 32 or 64 bits. Try this:

```
>>> 2**256
115792089237316195423570985008687907853269984665640564039457584007913
129639936
```

Large numbers work. They may be a bit slow, but they work perfectly fine.

Rational numbers

Rational numbers are not commonly used. They must be imported from the standard library. We must import the `fractions.Fraction` class definition. It looks like this:

```
>>> from fractions import Fraction
```

Once we have the `Fraction` class defined, we can use it to create numbers. Let's say we were sent out to track down a missing device. Details of the device are strictly need-to-know. Since we're new agents, all that HQ will release to us is the overall size in square inches.

Here's an exact calculation of the area of a device we found. It is measured as 4⅞" multiplied by 2¼":

```
>>> length=4+Fraction("7/8")
>>> width=2+Fraction("1/4")
>>> length*width
Fraction(351, 32)
```

Okay, the area is 351/32, which is—what?—in real inches and fractions.

We can use Python's `divmod()` function to work this out. The `divmod()` function gives us a quotient and a remainder, as shown in the following code:

```
>>> divmod(351,32)
(10, 31)
```

It's about 5 × 2, so the value seems to fit within our rough approximation. We can transmit that as the proper result. If we found the right device, we'll be instructed on what to do with it. Otherwise, we might have blown the assignment.

Floating-point numbers

We can write floating-point values in common or scientific notation as follows:

```
3.1415926
6.22E12
```

The presence of the decimal point distinguishes an integer from a float.

These are ordinary double-precision floating-point numbers. It's important to remember that floating-point values are only approximations. They usually have a 64-bit implementation.

If you're using CPython, they're explicitly based on the C compiler that was shown in the `sys.version` startup message. We can also get information from the `platform` package as shown in the following code snippet:

```
>>> import platform
>>> platform.python_build()
('v3.3.4:7ff62415e426', 'Feb  9 2014 00:29:34')
>>> platform.python_compiler()
'GCC 4.2.1 (Apple Inc. build 5666) (dot 3)'
```

This tells us which compiler was used. That, in turn, can tell us what floating-point libraries were used. This may help determine which underlying mathematical libraries are in use.

Decimal numbers

We need to be careful with money. *Words to live by: the accountants watching over spies are a tight-fisted bunch.*

What's important is that floating-point numbers are an approximation. We can't rely on approximations when working with money. For currency, we need exact decimal values, nothing else will do. Decimal numbers can be used with the help of an extension module. We'll import the `decimal.Decimal` class definition to work with currency. It looks like this:

```
>>> from decimal import Decimal
```

The informant we bribed to locate the device wants to be paid 50,000 Greek Drachma for the information on the missing device. When we submit our expenses, we'll need to include everything, including the cab fare (23.50 dollars) and the expensive lunch we had to buy her (12,900 GRD).

Why wouldn't the informant accept Dollars or Euros? We don't want to know, we just want their information. Recently, Greek Drachma were trading at 247.616 per dollar.

What's the exact budget for the information? In drachma and dollars?

First, we will convert currency exact to the mil (1000 of a dollar):

```
>>> conversion=Decimal("247.616")
>>> conversion
Decimal('247.616')
```

The tab for our lunch, converted from drachma to dollars, is calculated as follows:

```
>>> lunch=Decimal("12900")
>>> lunch/conversion
Decimal('52.09679503747738433703799431')
```

What? How is that mess going to satisfy the accountants?

All those digits are a consequence of exact division: we get a lot of decimal places of precision; not all of them are really relevant. We need to formalize the idea of *rounding off* the value so that the government accountants will be happy. The nearest penny will do. In the `Decimal` method, we'll use the `quantize` method. The term **quantize** refers to rounding up, rounding down, and truncating a given value. The `decimal` module offers a number of quantizing rules. The default rule is ROUND_HALF_EVEN: round to the nearest value; in the case of a tie, prefer the even value. The code looks as follows:

```
>>> penny=Decimal('.00')
>>> (lunch/conversion).quantize(penny)
Decimal('52.10')
That's much better. How much was the bribe we needed to pay?
>>> bribe=50000
>>> (bribe/conversion).quantize(penny)
Decimal('201.93')
```

Notice that the division involved an integer and a decimal. Python's definition of decimal will quietly create a new decimal number from the integer so that the math will be done using decimal objects.

The cab driver charged us US Dollars. We don't need to do much of a conversion. So, we will add this amount to the final amount, as shown in the following code:

```
>>> cab=Decimal('23.50')
That gets us to the whole calculation: lunch plus bribe, converted,
plus cab.
>>> ((lunch+bribe)/conversion).quantize(penny)+cab
Decimal('277.52')
```

Wait. We seem to be off by a penny. Why didn't we get 277.53 dollars as an answer?

Rounding. The basic rule is called *round half up*. Each individual amount (52.10 and 201.93) had a fraction of a penny value rounded up. (The more detailed values were 52.097 and 201.926.) When we computed the sum of the drachma before converting, the total didn't include the two separately rounded-up half-penny values.

We have a very fine degree of control over this. There are a number of rounding schemes, and there are a number of ways to define when and how to round. Also, some algebra may be required to see how it all fits together.

Complex numbers

We also have complex numbers in Python. They're written with two parts: a real and an imaginary value, as shown in the following code:

```
>>> 2+3j
(2+3j)
```

If we mix complex values with most other kinds of numbers, the results will be complex. The exception is decimal numbers. But why would we be mixing engineering data and currency? If any mission involves scientific and engineering data, we have a way to deal with the complex values.

Outside the numbers

Python includes a variety of data types, which aren't numbers. In the *Handling text and strings* section, we'll look at Python strings. We'll look at collections in *Chapter 2, Acquiring Intelligence Data*.

Boolean values, `True` and `False`, form their own little domain. We can extract a Boolean value from most objects using the `bool()` function. Here are some examples:

```
>>> bool(5)
True
>>> bool(0)
False
>>> bool('')
False
>>> bool(None)
False
>>> bool('word')
True
```

The general pattern is that most objects have a value `True` and a few exceptional objects have a value `False`. Empty collections, `0`, and `None` have a value `False`. Boolean values have their own special operators: `and`, `or`, and `not`. These have an additional feature. Here's an example:

```
>>> True and 0
0
>>> False and 0
False
```

When we evaluate `True and 0`, both sides of the `and` operator are evaluated; the right-hand value was the result. But when we evaluated `False and 0`, only the left-hand side of `and` was evaluated. Since it was already `False`, there was no reason to evaluate the right-hand side.

The `and` and `or` operators are *short-circuit* operators. If the left side of `and` is `False`, that's sufficient and the right-hand side is ignored. If the left-hand side of `or` is `True`, that's sufficient and the right-hand side is ignored.

Python's rules for evaluation follow mathematic practice closely. Arithmetic operations have the highest priority. Comparison operators have a lower priority than arithmetic operations. The logical operators have a very low priority. This means that `a+2 > b/3 or c==15` will be done in phases: first the arithmetic, then the comparison, and finally the logic.

Mathematical rules are followed by arithmetic rules. `**` has a higher priority than `*`, `/`, `//`, or `%`. The `+` and `-` operators come next. When we write `2*3+4`, the `2*3` operation must be performed first. The bit fiddling is even lower in priority. When you have a sequence of operations of the same priority (`a+b+c`), the computations are performed from left to right. If course, if there's any doubt, it's sensible to use parenthesis.

Assigning values to variables

We've been using the REPL feature of our Python toolset. In the long run, this isn't ideal. We'll be much happier writing scripts. The point behind using a computer for intelligence gathering is to automate data collection. Our scripts will require assignment to variables. It will also require explicit output and input.

We've shown the simple, obvious assignment statement in several examples previously. Note that we don't declare variables in Python. We simply assign values to variables. If the variable doesn't exist, it gets created. If the variable does exist, the previous value is replaced.

Let's look at some more sophisticated technology for creating and changing variables. We have multiple assignment statements. The following code will assign values to several variables at once:

```
>>> length, width = 2+Fraction(1,4), 4+Fraction(7,8)
>>> length
Fraction(9, 4)
>>> width
Fraction(39, 8)
>>> length >= width
False
```

We've set two variables, `length` and `width`. However, we also made a small mistake. The length isn't the larger value; we've switched the values of `length` and `width`. We can swap them very simply using a multiple assignment statement as follows:

```
>>> length, width = width, length
>>> length
Fraction(39, 8)
>>> width
Fraction(9, 4)
```

This works because the right-hand side is computed in its entirety. In this case, it's really simple. Then all of the values are broken down and assigned to the named variables. Clearly, the number of values on the right have to match the number of variables on the left or this won't work.

We also have *augmented* assignment statements. These couple an arithmetic operator with the assignment statement. The following code is an example of +=: using assignment augmented with addition. Here's an example of computing a sum from various bits and pieces:

```
>>> total= 0
>>> total += (lunch/conversion).quantize(penny)
>>> total += (bribe/conversion).quantize(penny)
>>> total += cab
>>> total
Decimal('277.53')
```

We don't have to write `total = total +`.... Instead, we can simply write `total +=` .... It's a nice clarification of what our intent is.

All of the arithmetic operators are available as augmented assignment statements. We might have a hard time finding a use for %= or **=, but the statements are part of the language.

The idea of a nice clarification should lead to some additional thinking. For example, the variable named `conversion` is a perfectly opaque name. Secrecy for data is one thing: we'll look at ways to encrypt data. Obscurity through shabby processing of that data often leads to a nightmarish mess. Maybe we should have called it something that defines more clearly what it means. We'll revisit this problem of obscurity in some examples later on.

Writing scripts and seeing output

Most of our missions will involve gathering and analyzing data. We won't be creating a very sophisticated **User Interface** (**UI**). Python has tools for building websites and complex **graphical user interfaces** (**GUIs**). The complexity of those topics leads to entire books to cover GUI and web development.

We don't want to type each individual Python statement at the >>> prompt. That makes it easy to learn Python, but our goal is to create programs. In GNU/Linux parlance, our Python application programs can be called **scripts**. This is because Python programs fit the definition for a *scripting* language.

For our purposes, we'll focus on scripts that use the **command-line interface** (**CLI**) Everything we'll write will run in a simple terminal window. The advantage of this approach is speed and simplicity. We can add graphic user interfaces later. Or we can expand the essential core of a small script into a web service, once it works.

What is an application or a script? A script is simply a plain text file. We can use any text editor to create this file. A word processor is rarely a good idea, since word processors aren't good at producing plain text files.

If we're not working from the >>> REPL prompt, we'll need to explicitly display the output. We'll display output from a script using the `print()` function.

Here's a simple script we can use to produce a receipt for bribing (*encouraging*) our informant.

From decimal import `Decimal`:

```
PENNY= Decimal('.00')

grd_usd= Decimal('247.616')
lunch_grd= Decimal('12900')
bribe_grd= 50000
cab_usd= Decimal('23.50')

lunch_usd= (lunch_grd/grd_usd).quantize(PENNY)
bribe_usd= (bribe_grd/grd_usd).quantize(PENNY)

print( "Lunch", lunch_grd, "GRD", lunch_usd, "USD" )
print( "Bribe", bribe_grd, "GRD", bribe_usd, "USD" )
print( "Cab", cab_usd, "USD" )
print( "Total", lunch_usd+bribe_usd+cab_usd, "USD" )
```

Let's break this script down so that we can follow it. Reading a script is a lot like putting a tail on an informant. We want to see where the script goes and what it does.

First, we imported the `Decimal` definition. This is essential for working with currency. We defined a value, `PENNY`, that we'll use to round off currency calculations to the nearest penny. We used a name in all caps to make this variable distinctive. It's not an ordinary variable; we should *never* see it on the left-hand side of an assignment statement again in the script.

We created the currency conversion factor, and named it `grd_usd`. That's a name that seems meaningful than `conversion` in this context. Note that we also added a small suffix to our amount names. We used names such as `lunch_grd`, `bribe_grd`, and `cab_usd` to emphasize which currency is being used. This can help prevent head-scrambling problems.

Given the `grd_usd` conversion factor, we created two more variables, `lunch_usd` and `bribe_usd`, with the amounts converted to dollars and rounded to the nearest penny. If the accountants want to fiddle with the conversion factor—perhaps they can use a different bank than us spies—they can tweak the number and prepare a different receipt.

The final step was to use the `print()` function to write the receipt. We printed the three items we spent money on, showing the amounts in GRD and USD. We also computed the total. This will help the accountants to properly reimburse us for the mission.

We'll describe the output as *primitive but acceptable*. After all, they're only accountants. We'll look into pretty formatting separately.

Gathering user input

The simplest way to gather input is to copy and paste it into the script. That's what we did previously. We pasted the Greek Drachma conversion into the script: `grd_usd= Decimal('247.616')`. We could annotate this with a comment to help the accountants make any changes.

Additional comments come at the end of the line, after a # sign. They look like this:

```
grd_usd= Decimal('247.616') # Conversion from Mihalis Bank 5/15/14
```

This extra text is part of the application, but it doesn't actually do anything. It's a note to ourselves, our accountants, our handler, or the person who takes over our assignments when we disappear.

This kind of data line is easy to edit. But sometimes the people we work with want more flexibility. In that case, we can gather this value as input from a person. For this, we'll use the input() function.

We often break user input down into two steps like this:

```
entry= input("GRD conversion: ")
grd_usd= Decimal(entry)
```

The first line will write a prompt and wait for the user to enter the amount. The amount will be a string of characters, assigned to the variable entry. Python can't use the characters directly in arithmetic statements, so we need to explicitly convert them to a useful numeric type.

The second line will try to convert the user's input to a useful Decimal object. We have to emphasize the try part of this. If the user doesn't enter a string that represents valid Decimal number, there will be a major crisis. Try it.

The crisis will look like this:

```
>>> entry= input("GRD conversion: ")
GRD conversion: 123.%$6
>>> grd_usd= Decimal(entry)
Traceback (most recent call last):
  File "<stdin>", line 1, in <module>
decimal.InvalidOperation: [<class 'decimal.ConversionSyntax'>]
```

Rather than this, enter a good number. We entered 123.%$6.

The bletch starting with Traceback indicates that Python raised an exception. A crisis in Python always results in an exception being raised. Python defines a variety of exceptions to make it possible for us to write scripts that deal with these kinds of crises.

Once we've seen how to deal with crises, we can look at string data and some simple clean-up steps that can make the user's life a little easier. We can't fix their mistakes, but we can handle a few common problems that stem from trying to type numbers on a keyboard.

Handling exceptions

An exception such as decimal.InvalidOperation is raised when the Decimal class can't parse the given string to create a valid Decimal object. What can we do with this exception?

We can ignore it. In that case, our application program crashes. It stops running and the agents using it are unhappy. Not really the best approach.

Here's the basic technique for catching an exception:

```
entry= input("GRD conversion: ")
try:
    grd_usd= Decimal(entry)
except decimal.InvalidOperation:
    print("Invalid: ", entry)
```

We've wrapped the `Decimal()` conversion and assignment in a `try:` statement. If every statement in the `try:` block works, the `grd_usd` variable will be set. If, on the other hand, a `decimal.InvalidOperation` exception is raised inside the `try:` block, the `except` clause will be processed. This writes a message and does not set the `grd_usd` variable.

We can handle an exception in a variety of ways. The most common kind of exception handling will clean up in the event of some failure. For example, a script that attempts to create a file might delete the useless file if an exception was raised. The problem hasn't been solved: the program still has to stop. But it can stop in a clean, pleasant way instead of a messy way.

We can also handle an exception by computing an alternate answer. We might be gathering information from a variety of web services. If one doesn't respond in time, we'll get a timeout exception. In this case, we may try an alternate web service.

In another common exception-handling case, we may reset the state of the computation so that an action can be tried again. In this case, we'll wrap the exception handler in a loop that can repeatedly ask the user for input until they provide a valid number.

These choices aren't exclusive and some handlers can perform combinations of the previous exception handlers. We'll look at the third choice, trying again, in detail.

Looping and trying again

Here's a common recipe for getting input from the user:

```
grd_usd= None
while grd_usd is None:
    entry= input("GRD conversion: ")
    try:
        grd_usd= Decimal(entry)
    except decimal.InvalidOperation:
        print("Invalid: ", entry)
print( grd_usd, "GRD = 1 USD" )
```

We'll add a tail to this and follow it around for a bit. The goal is to get a valid decimal value for our currency conversion, `grd_usd`. We'll initialize that variable as Python's special `None` object.

The `while` statement makes a formal declaration of our intent. We're going to execute the body of the `while` statement while the `grd_usd` variable remains set to `None`. Note that we're using the `is` operator to compare `grd_usd` to `None`. We're emphasizing a detail here: there's only one `None` object in Python and we're using that single instance. It's technically possible to tweak the definition of `==`; we can't tweak the definition of `is`.

At the end of the `while` statement, `grd_usd is None` must be `False`; we can say `grd_usd is not None`. When we look at the body of the statement, we can see that only one statement sets `grd_usd`, so we're assured that it must be a valid `Decimal` object.

Within the body of the `while` statement, we've used our exception-handling recipe. First, we prompt and get some input, setting the `entry` variable. Then, inside the `try` statement, we attempt to convert the string to a `Decimal` value. If that conversion works, then `grd_usd` will have that `Decimal` object assigned. The object will not be `None` and the loop will terminate. Victory!

If the conversion of entry to a `Decimal` value fails, the exception will be raised. We'll print a message, and leave `grd_usd` alone. It will still have a value of `None`. The loop will continue until a valid value is entered.

Python has other kinds of loops, we'll get to them later in this chapter.

Handling text and strings

We've glossed over Python's use of string objects. Expressions such as `Decimal('247.616')` and `input(GRD conversion: )` involve string literal values. Python gives us several ways to put strings into our programs; there's a lot of flexibility available.

Here are some examples of strings:

```
>>> "short"
'short'
>>> 'short'
'short'
>>> """A multiple line,
... very long string."""
'A multiple line,\nvery long string.'
>>> '''another multiple line
... very long string.'''
'another multiple line\nvery long string.'
```

We've used single quotes and apostrophes to create short strings. These must be complete within a single line of programming. We used triple quotes and triple apostrophes to create long strings. These strings can stretch over multiple lines of a program.

Note that Python echoes the strings back to us with a \n character to show the line break. This is called a **character escape**. The \ character escapes the normal meaning of n. The sequence \n doesn't mean n; \n means the often invisible newline character. Python has a number of escapes. The newline character is perhaps the most commonly used escape.

Sometimes we'll need to use characters which aren't present on our computer keyboards. For example, we might want to print one of the wide variety of Unicode special characters.

The following example works well when we know the Unicode number for a particular symbol:

```
>>> "\u2328"
'⌨'
```

The following example is better because we don't need to know the obscure code for a symbol:

```
>>> "\N{KEYBOARD}"
'⌨'
```

Converting between numbers and strings

We have two kinds of interesting string conversions: strings to numbers and numbers to strings.

We've seen functions such as Decimal() to convert a string to a number. We also have the functions: int(), float(), fractions.Fraction(), and complex(). When we have numbers that aren't in base 10, we can also use int() to convert those, as shown in the following code:

```
>>> int( 'dead', 16 )
57005
>>> int( '0b1101111010101101', 2 )
57005
```

We can create strings from numbers too. We can use functions such as hex(), oct(), and bin() to create strings in base 16, 8, and 2. We also have the str() function, which is the most general-purpose function to convert any Python object into a string of some kind.

More valuable than these is the `format()` method of a string. This performs a variety of value-to-string conversions. It uses a conversion format specification or template string to define what the resulting string will look like.

Here's an example of using `format()` to convert several values into a single string. It uses a rather complex format specification string:

```
>>> "{0:12s} {1:6.2f} USD {2:8.0f} GRD".format( "lunch", lunch_usd,
lunch_grd )
'lunch          52.10 USD    12900 GRD'
```

The format string has three conversion specifications: `{0:12s}`, `{1:6.2f}`, and `{2:8.0f}`. It also has some literal text, mostly spaces, but USD and GRD are part of the background literal text into which the data will be merged.

Each conversion specification has two parts: the item to convert and the format for that item. These two parts separated by a `:` inside `{}`. We'll look at each conversion:

- The item `0` is converted using the `12s` format. This format produces a twelve-position string. The string `lunch` was padded out to 12 positions.

- The item `1` is converted using the `6.2f` format. This format produces a six-position string. There will be two positions to the right of the decimal point. The value of `lunch_usd` was formatted using this.

- The item `2` is converted using an `8.0f` format. This format produces an eight-position string with no positions to the right of the decimal point. The value of `lunch_grd` was formatted using this specification.

We can do something like the following to improve our receipt:

```
receipt_1 = "{0:12s}                {1:6.2f} USD"
receipt_2 = "{0:12s} {1:8.0f} GRD {2:6.2f} USD"
print( receipt_2.format("Lunch", lunch_grd, lunch_usd) )
print( receipt_2.format("Bribe", bribe_grd, bribe_usd) )
print( receipt_1.format("Cab", cab_usd) )
print( receipt_1.format("Total", lunch_usd+bribe_usd+cab_usd) )
```

We've used two parallel format specifications. The `receipt_1` string can be used to format a label and a single dollar value. The `receipt_2` string can be used to format a label and two numeric values: one in dollars and the other in Greek Drachma.

This makes a better-looking receipt. That should keep the accountants off our back and let us focus on the real work: working on data files and folders.

Parsing strings

String objects can also be decomposed or parsed into substrings. We could easily write an entire chapter on all the various parsing methods that string objects offer. A common transformation is to strip extraneous whitespace from the beginning and end of a string. The idea is to remove spaces and tabs (and a few other nonobvious characters). It looks like this:

```
entry= input("GRD conversion: ").strip()
```

We've applied the `input()` function to get a string from the user. Then we've applied the `strip()` method of that string object to create a new string, stripped bare of whitespace characters. We can try it from the `>>>` prompt like this:

```
>>> "   123.45    ".strip()
'123.45'
```

This shows how a string with junk was pared down to the essentials. This can simplify a user's life; a few extra spaces won't be a problem.

Another transformation might be to split a string into pieces. Here's just one of the many techniques available:

```
>>> amount, space, currency = "123.45 USD".partition(" ")
>>> amount
'123.45'
>>> space
' '
>>> currency
'USD'
```

Let's look at this in detail. First, it's a multiple-assignment statement, where three variables are going to be set: `amount`, `space`, and `currency`.

The expression, `"123.45 USD".partition(" ")`, works by applying the `partition()` method to a literal string value. We're going to partition the string on the space character. The `partition()` method returns three things: the substring in front of the partition, the partition character, and the substring after the partition.

The actual partition variable may also be assigned an empty string, `' '`. Try this:

```
amount, space, currency = "word".partition(" ")
```

What are the values for `amount`, `space`, and `currency`?

If you use `help(str)`, you'll see all of the various kinds of things a string can do. The names that have __ around them map to Python operators. `__add__()`, for example, is how the + operator is implemented.

Organizing our software

Python gives us a number of ways to organize software into conceptual units. Long, sprawling scripts are hard to read, repair, or extend. Python offers us packages, modules, classes, and functions. We'll see different organizing techniques throughout our agent training. We'll start with function definition.

We've used a number of Python's built-in functions in the previous sections. Defining our own function is something we do with the def statement. A function definition allows us to summarize (and in some cases generalize) some processing. Here's a simple function we can use to get a decimal value from a user:

```
def get_decimal(prompt):
    value= None
    while value is None:
        entry= input(prompt)
        try:
            value= Decimal(entry)
        except decimal.InvalidOperation:
            print("Invalid: ", entry)
    return value
```

This follows the design we showed previously, packaged as a separate function. This function will return a proper Decimal object: the value of the value variable. We can use our get_decimal() function like this:

```
grd_usd= get_decimal("GRD conversion: ")
```

Python allows a great deal of variability in how argument values are supplied to functions. One common technique is to have an optional parameter, which can be provided using a keyword argument. The print() function has this feature, we can name a file by providing a keyword argument value.

```
import sys
print("Error", file=sys.stderr)
```

If we don't provide the file parameter, the sys.stdout file is used by default.

We can do this in our own functions with the following syntax:

```
def report( grd_usd, target=sys.stdout ):
    lunch_grd= Decimal('12900')
    bribe_grd= 50000
    cab_usd= Decimal('23.50')

    lunch_usd= (lunch_grd/grd_usd).quantize(PENNY)
    bribe_usd= (bribe_grd/grd_usd).quantize(PENNY)
```

```
    receipt_1 = "{0:12s}                  {1:6.2f} USD"
    receipt_2 = "{0:12s} {1:8.0f} GRD {2:6.2f} USD"
    print( receipt_2.format("Lunch", lunch_grd, lunch_usd),
file=target )
    print( receipt_2.format("Bribe", bribe_grd, bribe_usd),
file=target )
    print( receipt_1.format("Cab", cab_usd), file=target )
    print( receipt_1.format("Total", lunch_usd+bribe_usd+cab_usd),
file=target )
```

We defined our `report` function to have two parameters. The `grd_usd` parameter is required. The `target` parameter has a default value, so it's optional.

We're also using a global variable, PENNY. This was something we set outside the function. The value is usable inside the function.

The four `print()` functions provide the file parameter using the keyword syntax: `file=target`. If we provided a value for the `target` parameter, that will be used; if we did not provide a value for `target`, the default value of the `sys.stdout` file will be used. We can use this function in several ways. Here's one version:

```
rate= get_decimal("GRD conversion: ")
print(rate, "GRD = 1 USD")
report(rate)
```

We provided the `grd_usd` parameter value positionally: it's first. We didn't provide a value for the `target` parameter; the default value will be used.

Here's another version:

```
rate= get_decimal("GRD conversion: ")
print(rate, "GRD = 1 USD", file=sys.stdout)
report(grd_usd=rate, target=sys.stdout)
```

In this example, we used the keyword parameter syntax for both the `grd_usd` and `target` parameters. Yes, the `target` parameter value recapitulated the default value. We'll look at how to create our own files in the next section.

Working with files and folders

Our computer is full of files. One of the most important features of our operating system is the way it handles files and devices. Python gives us an outstanding level of access to various kinds of files.

However, we've got to draw a few lines. All files consist of bytes. This is a reductionist view that's not always helpful. Sometimes those bytes represent Unicode characters which makes reading the file is relatively easy. Sometimes those bytes represent more complex objects which makes reading the file may be quite difficult.

Pragmatically, files come in a wide variety of physical formats. Our various desktop applications (word processors, spread sheets, and so on) all have unique formats for the data. Some of those physical formats are proprietary products, and this makes them exceptionally difficult to work with. The contents are obscure (not secure) and the cost of ferreting out the information can be extraordinary. We can always resort to examining the low-level bytes and recovering information that way.

Many applications work with files in widely standardized formats. This makes our life much simpler. The format may be complex, but the fact that it conforms to a standard means that we can recover all of the data. We'll look at a number of standardized formats for subsequent missions. For now, we need to get the basics under our belts.

Creating a file

We'll start by creating a text file that we can work with. There are several interesting aspects to working with files. We'll focus on the following two aspects:

- Creating a `file` object. The `file` object is the Python view of an operating system resource. It's actually rather complex, but we can access it very easily.

- Using the file context. A file has a particular life: open, read or write, and then close. To be sure that we close the file and properly disentangle the OS resources from the Python object, we're usually happiest using a file as a context manager. Using a `with` statement guarantees that the file is properly closed.

Our general template, with `open("message1.txt", "w")` as target, for creating a file looks like this:

```
print( "Message to HQ", file=target )
print( "Device Size 10 31/32", file=target )
```

We'll open the file with the `open()` function. In this case, the file is opened in write mode. We've used the `print()` function to write some data into the file.

Once the program finishes the indented context of the `with` statement, the file is properly closed and the OS resources are released. We don't need to explicitly close the `file` object.

We can also use something like this to create our file:

```
text="""Message to HQ\n Device Size 10 31/32\n"""
with open("message1.txt", "w") as target:
    target.write(text)
```

Note the important difference here. The `print()` function automatically ends each line with a `\n` character. The `write()` method of a file object doesn't add anything.

In many cases, we may have more complex physical formatting for a file. We'll look at JSON or CSV files in a later section. We'll also look at reading and writing image files in *Chapter 3, Encoding Secret Messages with Steganography.*

Reading a file

Our general template for reading a file looks like this:

```
with open("message1.txt", "r") as source:
    text= source.read()
print( text )
```

This will create the `file` object, but it will be in read mode. If the file doesn't exist, we'll get an exception. The `read()` function will slurp the entire file into a single block of text. Once we're done reading the content of the file, we're also done with the `with` context. The file can be closed and the resources can be released. The text variable that we created will have the file's contents ready for further processing.

In many cases, we want to process the lines of the text separately. For this, Python gives us the `for` loop. This statement interacts with files to iterate through each line of the file, as shown in the following code:

```
with open("message1.txt", "r") as source:
    for line in source:
        print(line)
```

The output looks a bit odd, doesn't it?

It's double-spaced because each line read from the file contains a `\n` character at the end. The `print()` function automatically includes a `\n` character. This leads to double-spaced output.

We have two candidate fixes. We can tell the `print()` function not to include a `\n` character. For example, `print(line, end="")` does this.

A slightly better fix is to use the `rstrip()` method to remove the trailing whitespace from the right-hand end of line. This is slightly better because it's something we'll do often in a number of contexts. Attempting to suppress the output of the extra `\n` character in the `print()` function is too specialized to this one situation.

In some cases, we may have files where we need to filter the lines, looking for particular patterns. We might have a loop that includes conditional processing via the `if` statement, as shown in the following code:

```
with open("message1.txt", "r") as source:
    for line in source:
        junk1, keyword, size= line.rstrip().partition("Size")
        if keyword != '':
            print( size )
```

This shows a typical structure for text processing programs. First, we open the file via a `with` statement context; this assures us that the file will be closed properly no matter what happens.

We use the `for` statement to iterate through all lines of the file. Each line has a two-step process: the `rstrip()` method removes trailing whitespace, the `partition()` method breaks the line around the keyword `Size`.

The `if` statement defines a condition (`keyword != ''`) and some processing that's done only if the condition is `True`. If the condition is `False` (the value of `keyword` is `''`), the indented body of the `if` statement is silently skipped.

The assignment and `if` statements form the body of the `for` statement. These two statements are executed once for every line in the file. When we get to the end of the `for` statement, we can be assured that all lines were processed.

We have to note that we can create an exception to the usual *for all lines* assumption about processing files with the `for` statement. We can use the `break` statement to exit early from the loop, breaking the usual assumption. We'd prefer to avoid the `break` statement, making it easy to see that a `for` statement works for all lines of a file.

At the end of the `for` statement, we're done processing the file. We're done with the `with` context, too. The file will be closed.

Defining more complex logical conditions

What if we have more patterns than what we're looking for? What if we're processing more complex data?

Let's say we've got something like this in a file:

```
Message to Field Agent 006 1/2
Proceed to Rendezvous FM16uu62
Authorization to Pay $250 USD
```

We're looking for two keywords: `Rendezvous` and `Pay`. Python gives us the `elif` clause as part of the `if` statement. This clause provides a tidy way to handle multiple conditions gracefully. Here's a script to parse a message to us from the headquarters:

```python
amount= None
location= None
with open("message2.txt", "r") as source:
    for line in source:
        clean= line.lower().rstrip()
        junk, pay, pay_data= clean.partition("pay")
        junk, meet, meet_data= clean.partition("rendezvous")
        if pay != '':
            amount= pay_data
        elif meet != '':
            location= meet_data
        else:
            pass # ignore this line
print("Budget", amount, "Meet", location)
```

We're searching the contents in the file for two pieces of information: the rendezvous location and the amount we can use to bribe our contact. In effect, we're going to summarize this file down to two short facts, discarding the parts we don't care about.

As with the previous examples, we're using a `with` statement to create a processing context. We're also using the `for` statement to iterate through all lines of the file.

We've used a two-step process to clean each line. First, we used the `lower()` method to create a string in lowercase. Then we used the `rstrip()` method to remove any trailing whitespace from the line.

We applied the `partition()` method to the cleaned line twice. One partition looked for `pay` and the other partition looked for `rendezvous`. If the line could be partitioned on `pay`, the `pay` variable (and `pay_data`) would have values not equal to a zero-length string. If the line could be partitioned on `rendezvous`, then the `meet` variable (and `meet_data`) would have values not equal to a zero-length string. The `else, if` is abbreviated `elif` in Python.

If none of the previous conditions are true, we don't need to do anything. We don't need an `else:` clause. But we decided to include the `else:` clause in case we later needed to add some processing. For now, there's nothing more to do. In Python, the `pass` statement does nothing. It's a syntactic placeholder; a thing to write when we must write something.

Solving problems – recovering a lost password

We'll apply many of our techniques to writing a program to help us poke around inside a locked ZIP file. It's important to note that any competent encryption scheme doesn't encrypt a password. Passwords are, at worst, reduced to a hash value. When someone enters a password, the hash values are compared. The original password remains essentially unrecoverable except by guessing.

We'll look at a kind of brute-force password recovery scheme. It will simply try all of the words in a dictionary. More elaborate guessing schemes will use dictionary words and punctuation to form longer and longer candidate passwords. Even more elaborate guessing will include *leet speak* replacements of characters. For example, using `1337 sp3@k` instead of `leet speak`.

Before we look into how ZIP files work, we'll have to find a usable word corpus. A common stand-in for a corpus is a spell-check dictionary. For GNU/Linux or Mac OS X computers, there are several places a dictionary can be found. Three common places are: `/usr/dict/words`, `/usr/share/dict/words`, or possibly `/usr/share/myspell/dicts`.

Windows agents may have to search around a bit for similar dictionary resources. Look in `%AppData%\Microsoft\Spelling\EN` as a possible location. The dictionaries are often a `.dic` file. There may also be an associated `.aff` (affix rules) file, with additional rules for building words from the stem words (or lemmas) in the `.dic` file.

If we can't track down a usable word corpus, it may be best to install a standalone spell checking program, along with its dictionaries. Programs such as aspell, ispell, Hunspell, Open Office, and LibreOffice contain extensive collections of spelling dictionaries for a variety of languages.

There are other ways to get various word corpora. One way is to search all of the text files for all of the words in all of those files. The words we used to create a password may be reflected in words we actually use in other files.

Another good approach is to use the Python **Natural Language Toolkit (NLTK)**, which has a number of resources for handling natural language processing. As this manual was going to press, a version has been released which works with Python3. See `https://pypi.python.org/pypi/nltk`. This library provides lexicons, several wordlist corpora, and word stemming tools that are far better than simplistic spell-checking dictionaries.

Your mission is to locate a dictionary on your computer. If you can't find one, then download a good spell-check program and use its dictionary. A web search for `web2` (`Webster's Second International`) may turn up a usable corpus.

Reading a word corpus

The first thing we need to do is read our spell-check corpus. We'll call it a corpus—a body of words—not a dictionary. The examples will be based on **web2 (Webster's Second International) all 234,936 words worth**. This is generally available in BSD Unix and Mac OS X.

Here's a typical script that will examine a corpus:

```
count= 0
corpus_file = "/usr/share/dict/words"
with open( corpus_file ) as corpus:
    for line in corpus:
        word= line.strip()
        if len(word) == 10:
            print(word)
            count += 1
print( count )
```

We've opened the corpus file and read all of the lines. The word was located by stripping whitespace from the line; this removes the trailing \n character. An `if` statement was used to filter the 10-letter words. There are 30,878 of those, from abalienate to Zyzzogeton.

This little script isn't really part of any larger application. It's a kind of technology spike—something we're using to nail down a detail. When writing little scripts like this, we'll often skip careful design of classes or functions and just slap some Python statements into a file.

In POSIX-compliant OSes, we can do two more things to make a script easy to work with. First, we can add a special comment on the very first line of the file to help the OS figure out what to do with it. The line looks like this:

```
#!/usr/bin/env python3
```

This tells the OS how to handle the script. Specifically, it tells the OS to use the `env` program. The `env` program will then locate our installation of Python 3. Responsibility will be handed off to the `python3` program.

The second step is to mark the script as executable. We use the OS command, `chmod +x some_file.py`, to mark a Python file as an executable script.

If we've done these two steps, we can execute a script by simply typing its name at the command prompt.

In Windows, the file extension (`.py`) is associated with the Python program. There is an **Advanced Settings** panel that defines these file associations. When you installed Python, the association was built by the installer. This means that you can enter the name of a Python script and Windows will search through the directories named in your `PATH` value and execute that script properly.

Reading a ZIP archive

We'll use Python's `zipfile` module to work with a ZIP archive. This means we'll need to use `import zipfile` before we can do anything else. Since a ZIP archive contains multiple files, we'll often want to get a listing of the available files in the archive. Here's how we can survey an archive:

```
import zipfile
with zipfile.ZipFile( "demo.zip", "r" ) as archive:
    archive.printdir()
```

We've opened the archive, creating a file processing context. We then used the archive's `printdir()` method to dump the members of the archive.

We can't, however, extract any of the files because the ZIP archive was encrypted and we lost the password. Here's a script that will try to read the first member:

```
import zipfile
with zipfile.ZipFile( "demo.zip", "r" ) as archive:
    archive.printdir()
    first = archive.infolist()[0]
    with archive.open(first) as member:
        text= member.read()
        print( text )
```

We've created a file processing context using the open archive. We used the `infolist()` method to get information on each member. The `archive.infolist()` `[0]` statement will pick item zero from the list, that is, the first item.

We tried to create a file processing context for this specific member. Instead of seeing the content of the member, we get an exception. The details will vary, but your exception message will look like this:

```
RuntimeError: File <zipfile.ZipInfo object at 0x1007e78e8> is
encrypted, password required for extraction
```

The hexadecimal number (`0x1007e78e8`) may not match your output, but you'll still get an error trying to read an encrypted ZIP file.

Using brute-force search

To recover the files, we'll need to resort to brute-force search for a workable password. This means inserting our corpora reading loop into our archive processing context. It's a bit of flashy copy-and-paste that leads to a script like the following:

```python
import zipfile
import zlib
corpus_file = "/usr/share/dict/words"

with zipfile.ZipFile( "demo.zip", "r" ) as archive:
    first = archive.infolist()[0]
    print( "Reading", first.filename )
    with open( corpus_file ) as corpus:
        for line in corpus:
            word= line.strip().encode("ASCII")
            try:
                with archive.open(first, 'r', pwd=word) as member:
                    text= member.read()
                print( "Password", word )
                print( text )
                break
            except (RuntimeError, zlib.error, zipfile.BadZipFile):
                pass
```

We've imported two libraries: `zipfile` as well as `zlib`. We added `zlib` because it turns out that we'll sometimes see `zlib.error` exceptions when guessing passwords. We created a context for our open archive file. We used the `infolist()` method to get names of members and fetched just the first file from that list. If we can read one file, we can read them all.

Then we opened our corpus file, and created a file processing context for that file. For each line in the corpora, we used two methods of the line: the `strip()` method will remove the trailing `"\n"`, and the `encode("ASCII")` method will transform the line from Unicode characters to ASCII bytes. We need this because ZIP library passwords are ASCII bytes, not proper Unicode character strings.

The `try:` block attempts to open and read the first member. We created a file processing context for this member within the archive. We tried to read the member. If anything goes wrong while we are trying to read the encrypted member, an exception will be raised. The usual culprit, of course, is attempting to read the member with the wrong password.

If everything works well, then we guessed the correct password. We can print the recovered password, as well as the text of the member as a confirmation.

Note that we've used a `break` statement to end the corpora processing `for` loop. This changes the `for` loop's semantics from `for all` words to `there exists a word`. The `break` statement means the loop ends as soon as a valid password is found. No further words in the corpus need to be processed.

We've listed three kinds of exceptions that might be raised from attempting to use a bad password. It's not obvious why different kinds of exceptions may be raised by wrong passwords. But it's easy to run some experiments to confirm that a variety of different exceptions really are raised by a common underlying problem.

Summary

In this chapter, we saw the basics of our espionage toolkit: Python and our text editor of choice. We've worked with Python to manipulate numbers, strings, and files. We saw a number of Python statements: assignment, `while`, `for`, `if`, `elif`, `break`, and `def`. We saw how an expression (such as `print("hello world")`) can be used as a Python statement.

We also looked at the Python API for processing a ZIP file. We saw how Python works with popular file-archive formats. We even saw how to use a simple corpus of words to recover a simple password.

Now that we have the basics, we're ready for more advanced missions. The next thing we've got to do is start using the World Wide Web (WWW) to gather information and carry it back to our computer.

2
Acquiring Intelligence Data

We're going to acquire intelligence data from a variety of sources. We might interview people. We might steal files from a secret underground base. We might search the **World Wide Web (WWW)**, and this is what we'll focus on in this chapter. Using our own cameras or recording devices is the subject of the next chapter.

Important espionage targets include natural resources, popular opinion, and strategic economic strengths. This kind of background information is useful in a number of ways. A great deal of the world's data is already on the Web, and the rest will get there eventually. Any modern search for intelligence starts with the Web.

We can use Python libraries such as `http.client` and `urllib` to get data from remote servers and transfer files to other servers. Once we've found remote files of interest, we're going to need a number of Python libraries to parse and extract data from these libraries.

In *Chapter 1*, *Our Espionage Toolkit*, we looked at how we can peek inside a ZIP archive. We'll look inside other kinds of files in this chapter. We'll focus on JSON files, because they're widely used for web services APIs.

Along the way, we'll cover a number of topics:

- How to access online data from Python.
- The HTTP protocol and how to access websites from our applications.
- The FTP protocol and how to upload and download large volumes of bulk data.
- Many of the core Python data structures will include lists, tuples, dictionaries, and sets, and how we use these structures to organize and manage information.
- At the end of this chapter, we'll be able to build applications that access live, current, up-to-the-minute data from the Web. Once we've got the data, we can filter and analyze it to create useful intelligence assets.

Accessing data from the Internet

The WWW and Internet are based on a series of agreements called **Request for Comments (RFC)**. The RFCs define the standards and protocols to interconnect different networks, that is, the rules for internetworking. The WWW is defined by a subset of these RFCs that specifies the protocols, behaviors of hosts and agents (servers and clients), and file formats, among other details.

In a way, the Internet is a controlled chaos. Most software developers agree to follow the RFCs. Some don't. If their idea is really good, it can catch on, even though it doesn't precisely follow the standards. We often see this in the way some browsers don't work with some websites. This can cause confusion and questions. We'll often have to perform both espionage and plain old debugging to figure out what's available on a given website.

Python provides a variety of modules that implement the software defined in the Internet RFCs. We'll look at some of the common protocols to gather data through the Internet and the Python library modules that implement these protocols.

Background briefing – the TCP/IP protocols

The essential idea behind the WWW is the Internet. The essential idea behind the Internet is the TCP/IP protocol stack. The IP part of this is the internetworking protocol. This defines how messages can be routed between networks. Layered on top of IP is the TCP protocol to connect two applications to each other. TCP connections are often made via a software abstraction called a **socket**. In addition to TCP, there's also UDP; it's not used as much for the kind of WWW data we're interested in.

In Python, we can use the low-level `socket` library to work with the TCP protocol, but we won't. A socket is a file-like object that supports open, close, input, and output operations. Our software will be much simpler if we work at a higher level of abstraction. The Python libraries that we'll use will leverage the socket concept under the hood.

The Internet RFCs defines a number of protocols that build on TCP/IP sockets. These are more useful definitions of interactions between host computers (servers) and user agents (clients). We'll look at two of these: **Hypertext Transfer Protocol (HTTP)** and **File Transfer Protocol (FTP)**.

Using http.client for HTTP GET

The essence of web traffic is HTTP. This is built on TCP/IP. HTTP defines two roles: host and user agent, also called server and client, respectively. We'll stick to server and client. HTTP defines a number of kinds of request types, including GET and POST.

A web browser is one kind of client software we can use. This software makes GET and POST requests, and displays the results from the web server. We can do this kind of client-side processing in Python using two library modules.

The http.client module allows us to make GET and POST requests as well as PUT and DELETE. We can read the response object. Sometimes, the response is an HTML page. Sometimes, it's a graphic image. There are other things too, but we're mostly interested in text and graphics.

Here's a picture of a mysterious device we've been trying to find. We need to download this image to our computer so that we can see it and send it to our informant from http://upload.wikimedia.org/wikipedia/commons/7/72/IPhone_Internals.jpg.

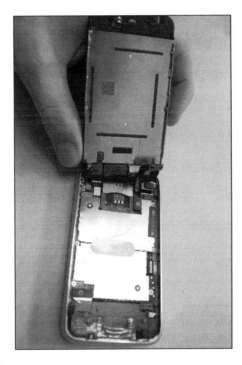

Here's a picture of the currency we're supposed to track down and pay with:

We need to download this image. Here is the link:

```
http://upload.wikimedia.org/wikipedia/en/c/c1/1drachmi_1973.jpg
```

Here's how we can use `http.client` to get these two image files:

```python
import http.client
import contextlib

path_list = [
    "/wikipedia/commons/7/72/IPhone_Internals.jpg",
    "/wikipedia/en/c/c1/1drachmi_1973.jpg",
]
host = "upload.wikimedia.org"

with contextlib.closing(http.client.HTTPConnection( host )) as connection:
    for path in path_list:
        connection.request( "GET", path )
        response= connection.getresponse()
        print("Status:", response.status)
        print("Headers:", response.getheaders())
        _, _, filename = path.rpartition("/")
        print("Writing:", filename)
        with open(filename, "wb") as image:
            image.write( response.read() )
```

We're using `http.client` to handle the client side of the HTTP protocol. We're also using the `contextlib` module to politely disentangle our application from network resources when we're done using them.

We've assigned a list of paths to the `path_list` variable. This example introduces list objects without providing any background. We'll return to lists in the *Organizing collections of data* section later in the chapter. It's important that lists are surrounded by `[]` and the items are separated by `,`. Yes, there's an extra `,` at the end. This is legal in Python.

We created an `http.client.HTTPConnection` object using the host computer name. This connection object is a little like a file; it entangles Python with operating system resources on our local computer plus a remote server. Unlike a file, an `HTTPConnection` object isn't a proper context manager. As we really like context managers to release our resources, we made use of the `contextlib.closing()` function to handle the context management details. The connection needs to be closed; the `closing()` function assures that this will happen by calling the connection's `close()` method.

For all of the paths in our `path_list`, we make an HTTP GET request. This is what browsers do to get the image files mentioned in an HTML page. We print a few things from each response. The status, if everything worked, will be 200. If the status is not 200, then something went wrong and we'll need to read up on the HTTP status code to see what happened.

 If you use a coffee shop Wi-Fi connection, perhaps you're not logged in. You might need to open a browser to set up a connection.

An HTTP response includes headers that provide some additional details about the request and response. We've printed the headers because they can be helpful in debugging any problems we might have. One of the most useful headers is `('Content-Type', 'image/jpeg')`. This confirms that we really did get an image.

We used `_, _, filename = path.rpartition("/")` to locate the right-most `/` character in the path. Recall that the `partition()` method locates the left-most instance. We're using the right-most one here. We assigned the directory information and separator to the variable `_`. Yes, `_` is a legal variable name. It's easy to ignore, which makes it a handy shorthand for *we don't care*. We kept the filename in the `filename` variable.

We create a nested context for the resulting image file. We can then read the body of the response—a collection of bytes—and write these bytes to the image file. In one quick motion, the file is ours.

The HTTP GET request is what underlies much of the WWW. Programs such as curl and wget are expansions of this example. They execute batches of GET requests to locate one or more pages of content. They can do quite a bit more, but this is the essence of extracting data from the WWW.

Changing our client information

An HTTP GET request includes several headers in addition to the URL. In the previous example, we simply relied on the Python http.client library to supply a suitable set of default headers. There are several reasons why we might want to supply different or additional headers.

First, we might want to tweak the User-Agent header to change the kind of browser that we're claiming to be. We might also need to provide cookies for some kinds of interactions. For information on the user agent string, see http://en.wikipedia. org/wiki/User_agent_string#User_agent_identification.

This information may be used by the web server to determine if a mobile device or desktop device is being used. We can use something like this:

```
Mozilla/5.0 (Macintosh; Intel Mac OS X 10_9_2) AppleWebKit/537.75.14
(KHTML, like Gecko) Version/7.0.3 Safari/537.75.14
```

This makes our Python request appear to come from the Safari browser instead of a Python application. We can use something like this to appear to be a different browser on a desktop computer:

```
Mozilla/5.0 (Macintosh; Intel Mac OS X 10.9; rv:28.0) Gecko/20100101
Firefox/28.0
```

We can use something like this to appear to be an iPhone instead of a Python application:

```
Mozilla/5.0 (iPhone; CPU iPhone OS 7_1_1 like Mac OS X)
AppleWebKit/537.51.2 (KHTML, like Gecko) Version/7.0 Mobile/11D201
Safari/9537.53
```

We make this change by adding headers to the request we're making. The change looks like this:

```
connection.request( "GET", path, headers= {
    'User-Agent':
        'Mozilla/5.0 (iPhone; CPU iPhone OS 7_1_1 like Mac OS X)
AppleWebKit/537.51.2 (KHTML, like Gecko) Version/7.0 Mobile/11D201
Safari/9537.53',
})
```

This will make the web server treat our Python application like it's on an iPhone. This might lead to a more compact page of data than might be provided to a full desktop computer that makes the same request.

The header information is a structure with the { key: value, } syntax. This is a dictionary. We'll return to dictionaries in the following *Organizing collections of data* section. It's important that dictionaries are surrounded by { }, the keys and values are separated by :, and each key-value pair is separated by , . Yes, there's an extra , at the end. This is legal in Python.

There are many more HTTP headers we can provide. The User-Agent header is perhaps most important to gather different kinds of intelligence data from web servers.

Using FTP in Python

FTP specifies ways to transfer files between computers. There are two principle variants: the original FTP and the more secure version, FTPS. This more secure version uses SSL to assure that the lower-level sockets are fully encrypted. It's sometimes called FTP_TLS, FTP with transport layer security.

The SSH standard includes a file-transfer protocol, SFTP. This is a part of SSH and is separate from other FTP variants. This is supported by the ftplib module, even though it's really a different protocol.

In some cases, FTP access is anonymous. No security credentials (such as usernames or passwords) are used. This is usually reserved for download-only content. Sometimes, anonymous access expects a placeholder username and password—the username should be *anonymous*, and typically, your e-mail address is used as a password. In other cases, we need to have proper credentials. We'll focus on publicly accessible FTP servers.

We're going to look for the CIA World Factbooks. We know that there are copies in Project Gutenberg. This leads us to use the ftp.ibiblio.org server as the target of our investigation. The base URL is ftp://ftp.ibiblio.org/pub/docs/books/gutenberg/.

FTP has its own language of commands used to examine remote (and local) filesystems, create and remove directories, as well as get and put files. Some of this language is exposed through the Python FTP module. Some of it is kept hidden under the hood.

We can see some top-level documents available on the Project Gutenberg server with a script like the following. Here's our initial step in discovering the data:

```
import ftplib

host = "ftp.ibiblio.org"
root = "/pub/docs/books/gutenberg/"

def directory_list( path ):
    with ftplib.FTP(host, user="anonymous") as connection:
        print("Welcome", connection.getwelcome())
        for name, details in connection.mlsd(path):
            print(name, details['type'], details.get('size'))
directory_list(root)
```

We imported the FTP library. We'll need this to do anything using the FTP protocol. We assigned the host, `host`, and root path, `root`, as strings. We'll use this in several functions that we need to define.

We defined a `directory_list()` function that will display names, types, and sizes from a directory. This lets us explore the files in our local directories. We'll use this function with different parameters after we've tracked down the directory with our candidate files.

The `directory_list()` function opens a context using a `ftplib.FTP` object. We don't need to use the `contextlib.closing()` function, because this context is well behaved. This object will manage the various sockets used to exchange data with the FTP server. One of the methods, `getwelcome()`, retrieves any welcome message. We'll see that this is pretty short. Sometimes, they're more elaborate.

We'll dump the top-level directory information that shows the various files, directories, and their sizes. The `details['type']` syntax is how we pick a particular name out of the name-value pairs in a dictionary. The `details.get('size')` syntax does a similar thing. Getting an item with `[]` will raise an exception if the name is not found. Getting an item with the `get()` method supplies a default value instead of an exception. Unless specified otherwise, the default value is `None`.

We're making the claim that the `details` dictionary must have a `type` item. If it doesn't, the program will crash, because something's very wrong. We're also making the claim that the `details` dictionary might or might not have the `size` item. If the size isn't present, the `None` value will do instead.

There are a number of files here. The `README` and `GUTINDEX.ALL` files look promising; let's examine them.

Downloading a file via FTP

The FTP library relies on a technique called a **callback function** to support incremental processing. Downloading a 13 MB file takes some time. Having our computer just doze off while downloading is impolite. It's good to provide some ongoing status with respect to progress (or lack of it thereof).

We can define callback functions in a number of ways. If we're going to use class definitions, the callback function will simply be another method of the class. Class definitions get a bit beyond the scope of our book. They're quite simple, but we have to focus on espionage, not software design. Here's a general-purpose get() function:

```python
import sys

def get( fullname, output=sys.stdout ):
    download= 0
    expected= 0
    dots= 0
    def line_save( aLine ):
        nonlocal download, expected, dots
        print( aLine, file=output )
        if output != sys.stdout:
            download += len(aLine)
            show= (20*download)//expected
            if show > dots:
                print( "-", end="", file=sys.stdout )
                sys.stdout.flush()
                dots= show
    with ftplib.FTP( host, user="anonymous" ) as connection:
        print( "Welcome", connection.getwelcome() )
        expected= connection.size( fullname )
        print( "Getting", fullname, "to", output, "size", expected )
        connection.retrlines( "RETR {0}".format(fullname), line_save )
    if output != sys.stdout:
        print() # End the "dots"
```

The get() function contains a function definition buried inside it. The line_save() function is the callback function that's used by the retrlines() function of an FTP connection. Each line of data from the server will be passed to the line_save() function to process it.

Our `line_save()` function uses three `nonlocal` variables: `download`, `expected`, and `dots`. These variables are neither global nor are they local to the `line_save()` function. They're initialized before any lines are downloaded, and they are updated within the `line_save()` function on a line-by-line basis. As they are a saved state for the `line_save()` function, we need to notify Python not to create local variables when these are used in an assignment statement.

The function's primary job is to print the line to the file named in the `output` variable. Interestingly, the `output` variable is also nonlocal. As we never try to assign a new value to this variable, we don't need to notify Python about its use in an assignment statement. A function has read access to nonlocal variables; write access requires special arrangements via the `global` or `nonlocal` statements.

If the output file is `sys.stdout`, we're displaying the file on the console. Writing status information is just confusing. If the output file is not `sys.stdout`, we're saving the file. Showing some status is helpful.

We compute how many dots (from 0 to 19) to show. If the number of dots has increased, we'll print another dash. Yes, we called the variable `dots` but decided to print dashes. Obscurity is never a good thing. You might want to take an independent mission and write your own version, which is clearer than this.

The `get()` function creates a context using an `ftplib.FTP` object. This object will manage the various sockets used to exchange data with the FTP server. We use the `getwelcome()` method to get the welcome message. We use the `size()` method to get the size of the file we're about to request. By setting the `expected` variable, we can assure that up to 20 dashes are displayed to show the state of the download.

The `retrlines()` method of the connection requires an FTP command and a callback function. It sends the command; each line of the response is sent to the callback function.

Using our FTP get() function

We can use this `get()` function to download files from the server. We'll start with two examples of extracting files from an FTP server:

```
# show the README on sys.stdout
get(root+"README")

# get GUTINDEX.ALL
with open("GUTINDEX.ALL", "w", encoding="UTF-8") as output:
    get(root+"GUTINDEX.ALL", output)
```

The first example is a small file. We'll display the README file, which might have useful information. It's usually small, and we can write it to stdout immediately. The second example will open a file processing context to save the large GUTINDEX. ALL file locally for further analysis. It's quite large, and we certainly don't want to display it immediately. We can search this index file for CIA World Factbooks. There are several Factbooks.

The introduction to the GUTINDEX.ALL file describes how document numbers turn into directory paths. One of the CIA World Factbooks, for example, is document number 35830. This becomes the directory path 3/5/3/35380/. The document will be in this directory.

We can use our directory_list() function to see what else is there:

```
directory_list( root+"3/5/8/3/35830/" )
```

This will show us that there are several subdirectories and a ZIP file that appears to have images. We'll start with the text document. We can use our get() function to download the CIA Factbook in a script like the following:

```
with open("35830.txt", "w", encoding="UTF-8") as output:
    get(root+"3/5/8/3/35830/"+"35830.txt", output)
```

This gets us one of the CIA World Factbooks. We can easily track down the others. We can then analyze information from these downloaded documents.

Using urllib for HTTP, FTP, or file access

The urllib package wraps HTTP, FTP, and local file access in a single, tidy package. In the most common situations, this package allows us to elide some of the processing details we saw in the previous examples.

The advantage of the general approach in urllib is that we can write smallish programs that can work with data from a wide variety of locations. We can rely on urllib to work with HTTP, FTP, or local files seamlessly. The disadvantage is that we can't do some more complex HTTP or FTP interactions. Here's an example of downloading two images with the urllib version of the HTTP get function:

```
import urllib.request

url_list = [
"http://upload.wikimedia.org/wikipedia/commons/7/72/IPhone_Internals.
jpg",
"http://upload.wikimedia.org/wikipedia/en/2/26/Common_face_of_one_
euro_coin.jpg",
    ]
```

```
for url in url_list:
    with urllib.request.urlopen( url ) as response:
        print( "Status:", response.status )
        _, _, filename = response.geturl().rpartition("/")
        print( "Writing:", filename )
        with open( filename, "wb" ) as image:
            image.write( response.read() )
```

We've defined two URLs. When using `urllib`, we can provide full URLs without having to distinguish between the host and the path we're tying to access.

We create a context using `urllib.request.urlopen()`. This context will contain all of the resources used for getting the file from the World Wide Web. The `response` object is called a **file-like object** in Python parlance. We can use it the way we'd use a file: it supports `read()` and `readline()` methods. It can be used in a `for` statement to iterate over lines of a text file.

Using urllib for FTP access

We can use a simple `urllib.request` to get a file via FTP. We can simply change the URL to reflect the protocol we're using. Something like this works well:

```
import sys
import urllib.request
readme= "ftp://ftp.ibiblio.org/pub/docs/books/gutenberg/README"
with urllib.request.urlopen(readme) as response:

    sys.stdout.write( response.read().decode("ascii") )
```

This will open the source file and print it on `sys.stdout`. Note that we had to decode the bytes from ASCII to create proper Unicode characters for use by Python. We can print the other status and header information if we find it necessary.

We can also use a local file URL. The schema is `file:` instead of `http:` or `ftp:`. Generally, the hostname is omitted, thus leading to file URLs like this:

```
local= "file:///Users/slott/Documents/Writing/Secret Agent's Python/
currency.html"
```

Using `urllib` leads to a few pleasant simplifications. We can treat resources located across the WWW with code that's similar to handling a local file. Remote resources are often slower than local files; we might want to give up waiting after a period of time. Also, there's the possibility of network disconnections. Our error handling needs to be more robust when working with remote data.

Using a REST API in Python

A great deal of intelligence data is available through REST APIs. Much of the data is available in simple JSON, CSV, or XML documents. In order to make sense of this data, we need to be able to parse these various kinds of serialization formats. We'll focus on JSON because it's widely used. Sadly, it's not universal.

A REST protocol is essentially HTTP. It will leverage POST, GET, PUT, and DELETE requests to implement the essential four stages in the life of persistent data: **Create, Retrieve, Update, and Delete (CRUD)** rules.

We'll look at currency conversion as a simple web API. This can both help us bribe our information sources as well as provide important information on the overall state of a nation's economy. We can measure national economies against each other as well as measure them against non-national crypto currencies such as bitcoins.

We'll get exchange and currency information from http://www.coinbase.com. There are a lot of similar services; this one seems reasonably complete. They seem to have up-to-date currency information that we can report to HQ as part of an overall intelligence assessment.

Their API documentation is available at https://coinbase.com/api/doc. This tells us what URLs to use, what data to provide with the URL, and what kind of response to expect.

Getting simple REST data

We can get the currency exchange data either with the http.client or urllib.request module. This won't be new to us; we already grabbed data using both libraries. The responses from this website will be in the JSON notation. For more information, see http://www.json.org/.

To parse a JSON document, we'll need to import the json module from the standard library. The response that we get from urllib is a sequence of bytes. We'll need to decode these bytes to get a string. We can then use the json.loads() function to build Python objects from that string. Here's how it looks:

```
import urllib.request
import json
query_currencies= "http://www.coinbase.com/api/v1/currencies/"
with urllib.request.urlopen( query_currencies ) as document:
    print(document.info().items())
    currencies= json.loads( document.read().decode("utf-8") )
    print(currencies)
```

We imported the two libraries that we need: `urllib.request` to get the data and `json` to parse the response.

The currency query (`/api/v1/currencies/`) is described in the API documentation on the Coinbase website. When we make this request, the resulting document will have all of the currencies they know about.

We printed `document.info().items()`; this is the collection of headers that came back with the response. Sometimes, these are interesting. In this case, they don't tell us too much that we don't already know. What's important is that the `Content-Type` header has a `application/json; charset=utf-8` value . This tells us how to decode the bytes.

We read the resulting document (`document.read()`) and then converted the bytes to characters. The `Content-Type` header says that the characters were encoded using `utf-8`, so we'll use `utf-8` to decode the bytes and recover the original sequence of characters. Once we have the characters, we can use `json.loads()` to create a Python object from the characters.

This will get us a list of currencies we can work with. The response object looks like this:

```
[['Afghan Afghani (AFN)', 'AFN'], ['Albanian Lek (ALL)', 'ALL'],
['Algerian Dinar (DZD)', 'DZD'], … ]
```

It is a list of lists that provides the names of 161 currencies.

In the next section, we'll look at ways to work with a list-of-tuple structure. Working with a list of list is going to be very similar to working with a list of tuple.

To make this more flexible, we need to turn the header `items()` list into a dictionary. From this, we can get the `Content-Type` value string from the dictionary. This string can be partitioned on `;` to locate the `charset=utf-8` substring. This string can subsequently be partitioned on the `=` character to locate the `utf-8` encoding information. This would be slightly better than assuming a `utf-8` encoding. The first step, creating a dictionary from the headers, has to wait until the *Organizing collections of data* section. First, we'll look at getting other information using the REST protocol.

Using more complex RESTful queries

Once we have a list of currencies, we can request spot conversion rates. This involves a somewhat more complex URL. We need to provide a currency code to get the current bitcoin exchange rate for that specific currency.

While it's not perfectly clear from the API documentation, the RFCs for the web state that we should encode the query string as part of our processing. In this specific situation, it doesn't seem possible for the query string to contain any characters that *require* encoding.

We're going to be fussy though and encode the query string properly using the `urllib` module. Encoding will be essential for a number of examples in *Chapter 4, Drops, Hideouts, Meetups, and Lairs*.

Query string encoding is done using the `urllib.parse` module. It looks like this:

```
scheme_netloc_path= "https://coinbase.com/api/v1/prices/spot_rate"
form= {"currency": currency}
query= urllib.parse.urlencode(form)
```

The `scheme_netloc_path` variable has a portion of the URL. It has the scheme (`http`), network location (`coinbase.com`), and path (`api/v1/prices/spot_rate`). This fragment of the URL doesn't have the query string; we'll encode this separately because it had dynamic information that changes from request to request.

Technically, a query string is a bunch of parameters that have been encoded so that certain reserved characters such as `?` and `#` don't cause any confusion to the web server. Pragmatically, the query string used here is very simple with only a single parameter.

To handle query strings in a general-purpose way, we defined an HTML form using a dictionary and assigned it to the `form` variable. This dictionary is a model of a form on an HTML web page with a single input field. We modeled an input field with a name, `currency`, that has an EUR value.

The `urllib.parse.urlencode()` function encodes all the fields of the form into a tidy representation with any reserved characters handled properly. In this case, there's only one field, and no reserved characters are used by the field name or the field value.

We can play with this in interactive Python:

```
>>> import urllib.parse
>>> form= {"currency": "EUR"}
>>> urllib.parse.urlencode(form)
'currency=EUR'
```

The preceding code shows how we built a form object as a dictionary and then encoded it to create a valid URL-encoded query string. As the data was so simple, the encoding is quite simple.

Here's an example with a more complex piece of data in the form:

```
>>> form['currency']= "Something with # or ?"
>>> urllib.parse.urlencode(form)
'currency=Something+with+%23+or+%3F'
```

First, we updated the form with different input; we changed the currency value to `Something with # or ?`. We'll look at dictionary updates in the next section. The updated value has reserved characters in it. When we encoded this form, the result shows how reserved characters are handled by URL encoding.

As we start working with more complex structures, we'll find that the built-in `print()` function isn't going to do everything we need. In the `pprint` module, the `pprint()` function does a much nicer job working with complex data. We can use this to get the pretty-print function:

```
import pprint
```

We can use our query template and the encoded data like this:

```
with urllib.request.urlopen( scheme_netloc_path+"?"+query ) as
document:
    pprint.pprint( document.info().items() )
    spot_rate= json.loads( document.read().decode("utf-8") )
```

The expression, `scheme_netloc_path+"?"+query`, assembled the complete URL from, the relatively static portions, and the dynamic query string. We've used a `with` statement to be sure that all of the network resources are properly released when we're done. We used the `pprint()` function to show the headers, which tell us the content type. The headers also include three cookies, which we're studiously ignoring for these examples.

When we print the `spot_rate` value, we see that the Python object looks like this:

```
{'currency': 'USD', 'amount': '496.02'}
Or this
{'currency': 'EUR', 'amount': '361.56'}
```

These are Python dictionary objects. We'll need to learn more about dictionaries to be able to work with these responses. Stay tuned for the *Using a Python dictionary mapping* section.

Saving our data via JSON

What if we want to save the data we downloaded? This is something in which JSON excels. We can use the JSON module to serialize objects into a string and write this string to a file.

Here's how we can save our two-spot currency rate pieces of data into a JSON document. First, we need to turn our `spot_rate` example from the *Getting more RESTful data* section into a function. Here's how it might look:

```
def get_spot_rate( currency ):
    scheme_netloc_path= "https://coinbase.com/api/v1/prices/spot_rate"
    form= {"currency":currency}
    query= urllib.parse.urlencode(form)

    with urllib.request.urlopen( scheme_netloc_path+"?"+query ) as
document:
        spot_rate= json.loads( document.read().decode("utf-8") )
    return spot_rate
```

This function requires the currency code as an argument. Given the currency code, it creates a tiny input form and encodes this to create the query string. In this case, we saved that string in the `query` variable.

We created the URL from a template and the data. This URL was used as a request to get a currency spot rate. We read the entire response and decoded the string from bytes. Once we had the string, we loaded a Python dictionary object using this string. We returned this dictionary using the `get_spot_rate()` function. We can now use this function to get some spot-rate dictionary objects:

```
rates = [
    get_spot_rate("USD"), get_spot_rate("GBP"),
    get_spot_rate("EUR") ]
```

This statement built a list-of-dictionary structure from our three spot-rate dictionaries. It assigned the collection to the `rates` variable. Once we have this, we can serialize it and create a file that has some useful exchange-rate information.

Here's how we use JSON to save a Python object to a file:

```
with open("rate.json","w") as save:
    json.dump( rates, save )
```

We opened a file to write something and used this as a processing context to be assured that the file will be properly closed when we're done. We then used the `json.dump()` function to dump our `rates` object to this file.

What's important about this is that JSON works most simply when we encode one object to a file. In this case, we built a list of individual objects and encoded that list into the file. As we can't easily perform any sort of partial or incremental encoding of objects into a JSON file, we built a list with everything in it. Except in cases of huge mountains of data, this technique of building and dumping a list works very nicely.

Organizing collections of data

We introduced some data collections earlier in the chapter. It's time to come clean on what these collections are and how we can use them effectively. As we observed in *Chapter 1, Our Espionage Toolkit*, Python offers a tower of different types of numbers. The commonly used numbers are built in; the more specialized numbers are imported from the standard library.

In a similar way, Python has a number of built-in collections. There is also a very large number of additional collection types available in the standard library. We'll look at the built-in lists, tuples, dictionaries, and sets. These cover the essential bases to work with groups of data items.

Using a Python list

The Python list class can be summarized as a mutable sequence. **Mutability** means that we can add, change, and remove items (the list can be changed). Sequence means that the items are accessed based on their positions within the list.

The syntax is pleasantly simple; we put the data items in `[]` and separate the items with `,`. We can use any Python object in the sequence.

HQ wants information on per capita consumption of selected cheese varieties. While HQ doesn't reveal much to field agents, we know that they often want to know about natural resources and strategic economic strengths.

We can find cheese consumption data at `http://www.ers.usda.gov/datafiles/Dairy_Data/chezcon_1_.xls`.

Sadly, the data is in a proprietary spreadsheet format and rather difficult to work with. To automate the data gathering, we would need something like Project Stingray to extract the data from this document. For manual data gathering, we can copy and paste the data.

Here's the data starting in 2000 and extending through 2010; we'll use it to show some simple list processing:

```
>>> cheese = [29.87, 30.12, 30.60, 30.66, 31.33, 32.62,
...     32.73, 33.50, 32.84, 33.02,]
>>> len(cheese)
10
>>> min(cheese)
29.87
>>> cheese.index( max(cheese) )
7
```

We created a list object and assigned it to the `cheese` variable. We used the `min()` function, which reveals the least value in the `29.87` sequence.

The `index()` method searches through the sequence for the matching value. We see that the maximum consumption found with the `max()` function has an index of `7` corresponding to 2007. After that, cheese consumption fell slightly.

Note that we have prefix function notations (`min()`, `max()`, `len()`, and several others). We also have method function notation, `cheese.index()`, and many others. Python offers a rich variety of notations. There's no fussy adherence to using only method functions.

As a list is mutable, we can append additional values to the list. We can use an `cheese.extend()` function to extend a given list with an additional list of values:

```
>>> cheese.extend( [32.92, 33.27, 33.51,] )
>>> cheese
[29.87, 30.12, 30.6, 30.66, 31.33, 32.62, 32.73, 33.5, 32.84, 33.02,
32.92, 33.27, 33.51]
```

We can also use the + operator to combine two lists.

We can reorder the data so that it's strictly ascending using the following code:

```
>>> cheese.sort()
>>> cheese
[29.87, 30.12, 30.6, 30.66, 31.33, 32.62, 32.73, 32.84, 32.92, 33.02,
33.27, 33.5, 33.51]
```

Note that the `sort()` method doesn't return a value. It mutates the list object itself; it doesn't return a new list. If we try something like `sorted_cheese= cheese.sort()`, we see that `sorted_cheese` has a `None` value. This is a consequence of `sort()` not returning a value; it mutates the list.

When working with time-series data, this kind of transformation will be confusing because the relationship between year and cheese consumption is lost when we sort the list.

Using list index operations

We can access individual items using the `cheese[index]` notation:

```
>>> cheese[0]
29.87
>>> cheese[1]
30.12
```

This allows us to pick specific items from a list. As the list was sorted, the item `0` is the least, and the item `1` is the next larger value. We can index *backwards* from the end of the list, as shown in the following code:

```
>>> cheese[-2]
33.5
>>> cheese[-1]
33.51
```

With the sorted data, the `-2` item is next to the largest one; the `-1` item is the last one, which is the largest value seen. In the original, unsorted `cheese[-2]` data would have been the 2009 data.

We can take a *slice* from a list too. Some common slice manipulations look like this:

```
>>> cheese[:5]
[29.87, 30.12, 30.6, 30.66, 31.33]
>>> cheese[5:]

[32.62, 32.73, 32.84, 32.92, 33.02, 33.27, 33.5, 33.51]
```

The first slice picks the first five values — the values of least cheese consumption. As we sorted the time-series data, we don't readily know which years' these were. We might need a more sophisticated data collection.

When working with collections, we find that we have a new comparison operator, `in`. We can use a simple `in` test to see if a value occurs anywhere in the collection:

```
>>> 30.5 in cheese
False
>>> 33.5 in cheese
True
```

The `in` operator works for tuples, dictionary keys, and sets.

The comparison operators compare the elements in order, looking for the first nonequal element between two sequences. Consider the following example:

```
>>> [1, 2, 1] < [1, 2, 2]
True
```

As the first two elements were equal, it was the third element that determined the relationship between the two lists. This rule also works for tuples.

Using a Python tuple

The Python tuple class can be summarized as an immutable sequence. Immutability means that once created, the tuple cannot be changed. The value of the number 3 is immutable, also: it's always 3. Sequence means that the items are accessed based on their positions within the tuple.

The syntax is pleasantly simple; we might need to put the data items in `()` and must separate the items with `,`. We can use any Python objects in the sequence. The idea is to create an object that looks like a mathematical coordinate: `(3, 4)`.

Tuples are used under the hood at many places within Python. When we use multiple assignments, for example, the right-hand side of the following code creates a tuple and the left-hand side decomposes it:

```
power, value = 0, 1
```

The right-hand side created a two-tuple `(0, 1)`. The syntax doesn't require `()` around the tuple. The left-hand side broke down a two-tuple, assigning the values to two distinct variables.

We generally use tuples for data objects where the number of elements is fixed by the problem domain. We often use tuples for coordinate pairs such as latitude and longitude. We don't need the flexible length that a list offers because the size of a tuple cannot change. What would a three-tuple mean when it's supposed to have just two values, latitude and longitude? A different kind of problem might involve longitude, latitude, and altitude; in this case, we're working with three-tuples. Using two-tuples or three-tuples in these examples is an essential feature of the problem: we won't be mutating objects to add or remove values.

When we looked at HTTP headers in requests and responses, we saw that these are represented as a list of two-tuples, such as (`'Content-Type'`, `'text/html; charset=utf-8'`). Each tuple has a header name (`'Content-Type'`) and header value (`'text/html; charset=utf-8'`).

Here's an example of using a two-tuple to include year and cheese consumption:

```
year_cheese = [(2000, 29.87), (2001, 30.12), (2002, 30.6), (2003,
30.66),
    (2004, 31.33), (2005, 32.62), (2006, 32.73), (2007, 33.5),
    (2008, 32.84), (2009, 33.02), (2010, 32.92), (2011, 33.27),
    (2012, 33.51)]
```

This list-of-tuple structure allows us to perform a slightly simpler analysis of the data. Here are two examples:

```
>>> max( year_cheese, key=lambda x:x[1] )
(2012, 33.51)
>>> min( year_cheese, key=lambda x:x[1] )
(2000, 29.87)
```

We applied the max() function to our list of tuples. The second argument to the max() function is another function—in this case, an anonymous lambda object—that evaluates just the second value in each tuple.

Here are two more examples that show what's happening with the lambda object:

```
>>> (2007, 33.5)[1]
33.5
>>> (lambda x:x[1])( (2007, 33.5) )
33.5
```

The (2007, 33.5) two-tuple has the [1] get item operation applied; this will pick the item at position 1, that is, the 33.5 value. The item at position zero is the year 2007.

The (lambda x:x[1]) expression creates an anonymous lambda function. We can then apply this function to the (2007, 33.5) two-tuple. As the x[1] expression picks the item at index position 1, we get the 33.5 value.

We can, if we want, create a fully defined, named function instead of using lambda, as shown in the following code

```
def by_weight( yr_wt_tuple ):
    year, weight = yr_wt_tuple
    return weight
```

A named function has two advantages: it has a name, and it can have multiple lines of code. A lambda function has the advantage of being tiny when the entire function can be reduced to a single expression.

We can use this technique to sort these two-tuples with a function instead of lambda, as shown in the following code snippet:

```
>>> by_cheese = sorted( year_cheese, key=by_weight )
>>> by_cheese
[(2000, 29.87), (2001, 30.12), (2002, 30.6), (2003, 30.66), (2004,
31.33), (2005, 32.62), (2006, 32.73), (2008, 32.84), (2010, 32.92),
(2009, 33.02), (2011, 33.27), (2007, 33.5), (2012, 33.51)]
```

We used a separate function to create a sorted copy of a sequence. The `sorted()` function requires an iterable item (the `year_cheese` list in this case) and a key function; it creates a new list from the old sequence that is sorted into order by the key function. In this case, our key function is the named function, `by_weight()`. Unlike the `list.sort()` method, the `sorted()` function does not modify the original sequence; the new list contains references to the original items.

Using generator expressions with list of tuples

If we want to locate cheese production for a given year, we need to search this sequence of two-tuples for the matching year. We can't simply use the `list.index()` function to locate an item, as we're only using part of the item. One strategy is to extract the year from the list using a generator expression, as shown in the following code:

```
>>> years = [ item[0] for item in year_cheese ]
>>> years
[2000, 2001, 2002, 2003, 2004, 2005, 2006, 2007, 2008, 2009, 2010, 2011, 2012]
```

The `item[0] for item in year_cheese` expression is a generator. It iterates through the `year_cheese` list, assigning each item to the variable named `item`. The `item[0]` subexpression is evaluated for each value of `item`. This will decompose the two-tuples, returning a single value from each tuple. The result is collected into a resulting list and assigned to the `years` variable. We'll return to this in the *Transforming sequences with generator functions* section.

We can then use `years.index(2005)` to get the index for a given year, as shown in the following code:

```
>>> years.index(2005)
5
>>> year_cheese[years.index(2005)]
(2005, 32.62)
```

As `years.index(2005)` gives us the position of a given year, we can use `year_cheese[ years.index( 2005 ) ]` to get the `year-cheese` two-tuple for the year 2005.

This idea of mapping from year to cheese consumption is directly implemented by a Python dictionary.

The `in` operator and other comparison operators work for tuples in the same way they work for lists. They compare the target tuple to each tuple in the list using a simple item-by-item comparison between the items in the tuples.

Using a Python dictionary mapping

A dictionary contains a mapping from keys to values. The Python dictionary class can be summarized as a mutable mapping. Mutability means that we can add, change, and remove items. Mapping means that the values are accessed based on their keys. Order is not preserved in a mapping.

The syntax is pleasantly simple: we put the key-value pairs in { }, separate the key from the value with :, and separate the pairs with ,. The values can be any kind of Python object. The keys, however, suffer from a restriction—they must be immutable objects. As strings and numbers are immutable, they make perfect keys. A tuple is immutable and a good key. A list is mutable though, and can't be used as a key.

When we looked at creating an HTTP form data, in the *Getting more RESTful data* section, we used a mapping from field name to field value. We got back a response, which was a mapping from keys to values. The response looked like this:

```
>>> spot_rate= {'currency': 'EUR', 'amount': '361.56'}
>>> spot_rate['currency']
'EUR'
>>> spot_rate['amount']
'361.56'
>>> import decimal
>>> decimal.Decimal(spot_rate['amount'])
Decimal('361.56')
```

After creating the `spot_rate` dictionary, we used the `dict[key]` syntax to get values of two of the keys, `currency` and `amount`.

As a dictionary is mutable, we can easily change the values associated with the keys. Here's how we can create and modify a form:

```
>>> form= {"currency":"EUR"}
>>> form['currency']= "USD"
>>> form
{'currency': 'USD'}
```

We created the `form` variable as a small dictionary. We can use this to make one spot-rate query. We then changed the value in the `form` dictionary. We can use this updated form to make a second spot-rate query.

When getting a value, the key must exist; otherwise, we'll get an exception. As noted earlier, we can also use `dict.get(key, default)` to get values when a key might not exist in the dictionary. Here are several examples:

```
>>> spot_rate['currency']
'EUR'
>>> spot_rate['oops']
```

```
Traceback (most recent call last):
  File "<stdin>", line 1, in <module>
KeyError: 'oops'
>>> spot_rate.get('amount')
'361.56'
>>> spot_rate.get('oops')
>>> spot_rate.get('oops', '#Missing')
'#Missing'
```

First, we fetched the value mapped to the currency key. We tried to fetch a value mapped to the oops key. We got a KeyError exception because the oops key isn't in the spot_rate dictionary.

We did the same kinds of things using the get() method. When we executed spot_rate.get('amount'), the key-value pair existed, so the value was returned.

When we executed spot_rate.get('oops'), the key didn't exist; the default return value was None. Python doesn't print None values, so we don't see any obvious result from this. When we executed spot_rate.get('oops', '#Missing'), we provided a return value that is not None, which displayed something visible. The idea is that we can then do things like this to make a series of related queries:

```
for currency in 'USD', 'EUR', 'UAH':
    form['currency']=  currency
    data= urllib.parse.urlencode( form )
    ...etc...
```

The for statement includes a tuple of values: 'USD', 'EUR', 'UAH'. We aren't required to put () around the tuple in this particular case because the syntax is unambiguous.

Each value from the literal tuple is used to set the currency value in the form. We can then use the urllib.parse.urlencode() function to build a query string. We might be using this in a urllib.urlopen() function to get a current spot price for bitcoins in that currency.

Using the dictionary access methods

Other interesting methods of a dictionary mapping include the keys(), values(), and items() methods. Here are some examples:

```
>>> spot_rate.keys()
dict_keys(['amount', 'currency'])
>>> spot_rate.items()
dict_items([('amount', '361.56'), ('currency', 'EUR')])
>>> spot_rate.values()
dict_values(['361.56', 'EUR'])
```

The keys() method gave us a dict_keys object, which contains just the keys in a simple list. We can sort this list or do other processing outside the dictionary. Similarly, the values() method gave us a dict_values object, which contains just the values in a simple list.

The items() method gave us a sequence of two-tuples, as shown in the following code:

```
>>> rate_as_list= spot_rate.items()
>>> rate_as_list
dict_items([('amount', '361.56'), ('currency', 'EUR')])
```

We created the rate_as_list variable from the spot_rate.items() list of two-tuples. We can easily convert a list of two-tuple to a dictionary using the dict() function and vice versa, as shown in the following code:

```
>>> dict(rate_as_list)
{'amount': '361.56', 'currency': 'EUR'}
```

This gives us a way to deal with the 161 currencies. We'll look at this in the next section, *Transforming sequences with generator functions*.

Note that the in operator works against the dictionary keys, not the values:

```
>>> 'currency' in spot_rate
True
>>> 'USD' in spot_rate
False
```

The currency key exists in the spot_rate dictionary. The USD value is not checked by the in operator. If we're looking for a specific value, we have to use the values() method explicitly:

```
'USD' in spot_rate.values()
```

Other comparison operators don't really make sense for a dictionary. It's essential to explicitly compare a dictionary's keys, values, or items.

Transforming sequences with generator functions

The data at http://www.coinbase.com/api/v1/currencies/, which was a RESTful request, was a giant list of lists. It started like this:

```
>>> currencies = [['Afghan Afghani (AFN)', 'AFN'], ['Albanian Lek
(ALL)', 'ALL'],
... ['Algerian Dinar (DZD)', 'DZD'],
... ]
```

If we apply the `dict()` function to this list of lists, we'll build a dictionary. However, this dictionary isn't what we want; the following code is how it looks:

```
>>> dict(currencies)
{'Afghan Afghani (AFN)': 'AFN', 'Albanian Lek (ALL)': 'ALL', 'Algerian
Dinar (DZD)': 'DZD'}
```

The keys in this dictionary are long `country currency (code)` strings. The values are the three-letter currency code.

We might want the keys of this as a handy lookup table for a person's reference to track down the proper currency for a given country. We might use something like this:

```
>>> dict(currencies).keys()
dict_keys(['Afghan Afghani (AFN)', 'Albanian Lek (ALL)', 'Algerian
Dinar (DZD)'])
```

This shows how we can create a dictionary from a list of lists and then extract just the `keys()` from this dictionary. This is, in a way, an excessive amount of processing for a simple result.

We showed an example of picking up some data using a generator function in the *Using a Python tuple* section. Here's how we'd apply it to this problem. We'll create a list comprehension using a generator function. The generator, surrounded by `[]`, will lead to a new list object, as shown in the following code:

```
>>> [name for name, code in currencies]
['Afghan Afghani (AFN)', 'Albanian Lek (ALL)', 'Algerian Dinar (DZD)']
```

The `currencies` object is the original list of lists. The real one has 161 items; we're working with a piece of it here to keep the output small.

The generator expression has three clauses. These are *subexpressions* for *targets* in *source*. The `[]` characters are separate punctuations used to create a list objects from the generated values; they're not part of the generator expression itself. The *subexpression* is evaluated for each target value. The *target* variable is assigned to each element from the *source* iterable object. Each two-tuple from the currencies list is assigned to the `name` and `code` target variables. The subexpression is just `name`. We can use this to build a dictionary from currency to full name:

```
>>> codes= dict( (code,name) for name,code in currencies )
>>> codes
{'DZD': 'Algerian Dinar (DZD)', 'ALL': 'Albanian Lek (ALL)', 'AFN':
'Afghan Afghani (AFN)'}
>>> codes['AFN']
'Afghan Afghani (AFN)'
```

We used a generator function to swap the two elements of each item of the currency list. The targets were name and code; the resulting subexpression is the (code,name) two-tuple. We built a dictionary from this; this dictionary maps currency codes to country names.

Using the defaultdict and counter mappings

There are a number of sophisticated mappings that are part of the standard library. Two of these are the defaultdict and Counter mappings. The defaultdict allows us to work more flexibly with keys that don't exist.

Let's look at the word corpus we used to recover a ZIP file password. We can use this word corpus for other purposes. One of the things that can help the crypto department decode messages is knowledge of two-letter sequences (digram or bigram) that occur commonly in the source documents.

What are the most common two-letter digrams in English? We can easily gather this from our dictionary, as shown in the following code:

```
from collections import defaultdict
corpus_file = "/usr/share/dict/words"
digram_count = defaultdict( int )
with open( corpus_file ) as corpus:
    for line in corpus:
        word= line.lower().strip()
        for position in range(len(word)-1):
            digram= word[position:position+2]
            digram_count[digram] += 1
```

We need to import the defaultdict class from the collections module because it's not built in. We created an empty defaultdict object, digram_count, using int as the initialization function. The initialization function handles missing keys; we'll look at the details in the following section.

We opened our word corpus. We iterated through each line in corpus. We transformed each line into a word by stripping the trailing spaces and mapping it to lowercase. We used the range() function to generate a sequence of positions from zero to one less than the length of the word (len(word)-1). We can pluck a two-character digram from each word using the word[position:position+2] slice notation.

When we evaluate digram_count[digram], one of two things will happen:

- If the key exists in the mapping, the value is returned, just like any ordinary dictionary. We can then add one to the value that is returned, thus updating the dictionary.

- If the key does not exist in this mapping, then the initialization function is evaluated to create a default value. The value of int() is 0, which is ideal to count things. We can then add 1 to this value and update the dictionary.

The cool feature of a defaultdict class is that no exception is raised for a missing key value. Instead of raising an exception, the initialization function is used.

This defaultdict(int) class is so common that we can use the Counter class definition for this. We can make two tiny changes to the previous example. The first change is as follows:

```
from collections import Counter
```

The second change is as follows:

```
digram_count= Counter()
```

The reason for making this change is that Counter classes do some additional things. In particular, we often want to know the most common counts, as shown in the following code:

```
>>> print( digram_count.most_common( 10 ) )
[('er', 42507), ('in', 33718), ('ti', 31684), ('on', 29811), ('te',
29443), ('an', 28275), ('al', 28178), ('at', 27276), ('ic', 26517),
('en', 25070)]
```

The most_common() method of a Counter object returns the counts in the descending order. This shows us that er is the most common English-language digram. This information might help the decoders back at HQ.

Using a Python set

The Python set class is mutable; we can add, change, and remove items. Items are either present or absent. We don't use positions or keys; we merely add, remove, or test the items. This means that sets have no inherent order.

The syntax is pleasantly simple; we put the data items in {} and separated the items with ,. We can use any immutable Python objects in the set. It's important to note that the items must be immutable—we can include strings, numbers, and tuples. We can't include a list or dictionary in a set.

As the {} characters are used both by dictionaries and sets, it's unclear what the empty pair, {}, means. Is this an empty dictionary or an empty set? It's much more clear if we use dict() to mean an empty dictionary and set() to mean an empty set.

A set is a simple collection of things; it is perhaps the simplest possible collection of things.

In looking at the digrams, we noticed that there were some digrams, including a - character. How many hyphenated words are in the dictionary? This is a simple set processing example:

```
corpus_file = "/usr/share/dict/words"
hyphenated = set()
with open( corpus_file ) as corpus:
    for line in corpus:
        word= line.lower().strip()
        if '-' in word:
            hyphenated.add(word)
```

We created an empty set and assigned it to the hyphenated variable. We checked each word in our collection of words to see if the - character is in the collection of characters. If we find the hyphen, we can add this word to our set of hyphenated words.

The word corpus on the author's computer had two hyphenated words. This raises more questions than it answers.

The in operator is essential for working with sets. The comparison operators implement subset and superset comparisons between two sets. The a <= b operation asks if a is a subset of b, mathematically, $a \subseteq b$.

Using the for statement with a collection

The for statement is the primary tool to iterate through the items in a collection. When working with lists, tuples, or sets, the for statement will pleasantly assure that all values in the collection are assigned to the target variable, one at a time. Something like this works out nicely:

```
>>> for pounds in cheese:
...     print( pounds )
...
29.87
etc.
33.51
```

The for statement assigns each item in the cheese sequence to the target variable. We simply print each value from the collection.

When working with the list-of-tuples structures, we can do something a bit more interesting, as shown in the following code:

```
>>> for year, pounds in year_cheese:
...     print( year, pounds )
...
2000 29.87
etc.
2012 33.51
```

In this example, each two-tuple was decomposed, and the two values were assigned to the target variables, year and pounds.

We can leverage this when transforming a Count object into percentages. Let's look at our digram_count collection:

```
total= sum( digram_count.values() )
for digram, count in digram_count.items():
    print( "{:2s} {:7d} {:.3%}".format(digram, count, count/total) )
```

First, we computed the sum of the values in the collection. This is the total number of digrams found in the original corpus. In this example, it was 2,021,337. Different corpora will have different numbers of digrams.

The for statement iterates through the sequence created by digram_count.items(). The items() method produces a sequence of two-tuples with the key and value. We assign these to two target variables: digram and count. We can then produce a nicely formatted table of all 620 digrams, their counts, and their relative frequency.

This is the kind of thing that the folks in the crypto department love.

When we apply the for statement to a dictionary directly, it iterates just over the keys. We could use something like this to iterate through the digram counts:

```
for digram in digram_count:
    print( digram, digram_count[digram], digram_count[digram]/total )
```

The target variable, digram, is assigned to each key. We can then use a syntax such as digram_count[digram] to extract the value for this key.

Using Python operators on collections

Some of the mathematical operators work with collections. We can use the + and *
operators with sequences such as lists and tuples, as shown in the following code:

```
>>> [2, 3, 5, 7] + [11, 13, 17]
[2, 3, 5, 7, 11, 13, 17]
>>> [2, 3, 5, 7] * 2
[2, 3, 5, 7, 2, 3, 5, 7]
>>> [0]*10
[0, 0, 0, 0, 0, 0, 0, 0, 0, 0]
```

These examples showed how we can concatenate two lists and multiply a list to
create a longer list with multiple copies of the original list. The `[0]*10` statement
shows a more useful technique to initialize a list to a fixed number of values.

Sets have a number of operators for union (|), intersection (&), difference (-), and
symmetric difference (^). Also, the comparison operators are redefined to work as
subset or superset comparisons. Here are some examples:

```
>>> {2, 3, 5, 7} | {5, 7, 11, 13, 17}
{2, 3, 5, 7, 11, 13, 17}
>>> {2, 3, 5, 7} & {5, 7, 11, 13, 17}
{5, 7}
>>> {2, 3, 5, 7} - {5, 7, 11, 13, 17}
{2, 3}
>>> {2, 3, 5, 7} ^ {5, 7, 11, 13, 17}
{2, 3, 11, 13, 17}
>>> {2, 3} <= {2, 5, 7, 3, 11}
True
```

The union operator, |, combines the two sets. A set means an element only occurs
once, so there are no duplicated elements in the union of the sets. The intersection of
two sets, &, is the set of common elements in the two sets. The subtraction operator,
-, removes elements from the set on the left-hand side. The symmetric difference
operator, ^, creates a new set that has elements which are in one or the other set but
not both; essentially, it is the same as an exclusive OR.

We showed just one comparison operator, the `<=` subset operator, between two sets.
The other comparison operators perform just as can be expected.

Solving problems – currency conversion rates

The problem we have is that our informants are always asking for odd or unusual currencies. This isn't really all that surprising; we're dealing with spies and criminals on the run. They always seem to need obscure foreign currencies for their own nefarious projects.

We can get a big pile of international exchange rates using a piece of code like the following:

```
query_exchange_rates= "http://www.coinbase.com/api/v1/currencies/
exchange_rates/"

with urllib.request.urlopen( query_exchange_rates ) as document:
    pprint.pprint( document.info().items() )
    exchange_rates= json.loads( document.read().decode("utf-8") )
```

The query string is a simple URL. When we make the request, we get back a long string of bytes. We decode this to make a proper string and use `json.loads()` to build a Python object.

The problem is that we get a giant dictionary object that's not really all that useful. It looks like this:

```
{'aed_to_btc': '0.000552',
 'aed_to_usd': '0.272246',
 'afn_to_btc': '3.6e-05',
 'afn_to_usd': '0.01763',
```

Also, it goes on and on for 632 different combinations of currencies.

The keys to this mapping involve two currencies separated by _to_ and written in lowercase letters. The currency code pieces that we got in the earlier example (see the *Using a REST API in Python* section) are in uppercase. We got a bit of work on our hands to match this data up properly.

We need to break this long list of currencies down into sublists. The neat way to handle this is with a dictionary of lists. We can use the `defaultdict` class to build these lists. Here's a typical approach:

```
from collections import defaultdict
rates = defaultdict(list)
for conversion, rate in exchange_rates.items():
    source, _, target = conversion.upper().partition("_TO_")
    rates[source].append( (target, float(rate)) )
```

We set the `rates` variable to be a `defaultdict(list)` object. When a key is not found in this dictionary, an empty list will be built as the value for that missing key.

We can iterate through each conversion and rate in the `items()` method of the raw data. We'll convert the conversion string to uppercase and then partition the conversion on the `_TO_` string. This will separate the two currency codes, assigning them to `source` and `target`. As they're uppercase, we can also match them against our list of currency-to-country codes.

We also converted the rate from a string to a more useful `float` number. The string isn't useful for further calculations.

We can then accumulate a list for each currency within the `rates` dictionary. If the `source` currency exists, we'll append it to the list that's already present in the dictionary. If the `source` currency doesn't exist, we'll create an empty list and append it to that empty list.

We'll append a target currency and the conversion rate as a simple two-tuple.

When we're done, we'll have tidy, short lists. Here's how we can pick a few currencies and display the conversions:

```
for c in 'USD', 'GBP', 'EUR':
    print( c, rates[c] )
```

For a select few currencies, we printed the currency and the list of conversion rates available right now.

This shows us results like the following:

```
GBP [('BTC', 0.003396), ('USD', 1.682624)]
EUR [('BTC', 0.002768), ('USD', 1.371864)]
```

The USD list is rather large, as it includes 159 other countries and currencies.

As we got the currency details from our earlier query, we can do this to make our output a little more useful:

```
currency_details = dict( (code,name) for name,code in currencies )
for c in 'USD', 'GBP', 'EUR':
    print( currency_details[c], rates[c] )
```

We built a dictionary that maps a currency code to the full name for the currency. When we look up the details for a currency, our output looks a little nicer, as shown in the following snippet:

```
British Pound (GBP) [('USD', 1.682624), ('BTC', 0.003407)]
Euro (EUR) [('USD', 1.371864), ('BTC', 0.002778)]
```

This is the kind of thing that can help us convert the bribe amounts into budget numbers that the accountants at HQ will find useful. We can also use this information to send national assessments based on the value of the local currency.

Also, we can use this for our own purposes to buy and sell bitcoins. This might help keep us one step ahead of international chaos. Alternatively, it may help us leverage the advantages of crypto currency.

We can save our currency details to a file using `json.dump(currency_details, some_open_file)`. See the example in the *Saving our data via JSON* section for a refresher on how this is done.

Summary

In this chapter, we saw the basics of using Python to access data available on the WWW. We used the HTTP protocol and the FTP protocol to transfer files around. We can use HTTPS and FTPS to assure that our data is kept secret.

We looked at using RESTful web services to gather data from information sources that have a defined API. RESTful web services are available for many kinds of data. They allow us to gather and analyze data from a variety of sources without a lot of tedious, error-prone pointing and clicking.

We also saw how to work with the various Python collections: lists, tuples, dictionaries, and sets. This gives us ways to capture and manage larger collections of information.

We looked at the JSON notation for Python objects. This is a handy way to transmit objects through the WWW. It's also handy for saving objects locally on our personal computer.

In the next chapter, we'll look at how we can work with image files. These are a bit more complex than JSON files, but the Python `pillow` package makes them easy to work with. We'll specifically use image files as a way to transmit hidden messages.

In *Chapter 4, Drops, Hideouts, Meetups, and Lairs*, we'll expand on the web services we saw in this chapter. We'll use geocoding web services and extract data from more complex online datasets.

3
Encoding Secret Messages with Steganography

We're going to acquire intelligence data from a variety of sources. In the previous chapter, we searched the WWW. We might use our own cameras or recording devices. We'll look at image processing and encoding in this chapter.

To work with images in Python, we'll need to install Pillow. This library gives us software tools to process image files. Pillow is a fork of the older PIL project; Pillow is a bit nicer to use than PIL.

Along the way, we'll visit some additional Python programming techniques, including:

- We'll review how Python works with OS files and also look at some common physical formats, including ZIP files, JSON, and CSV.

- We'll introduce JPEG files and learn to process them with Pillow. We'll have to install Pillow before we can make this work.

- We'll look at several image transformations, such as getting the EXIF data, creating thumbnails, cropping, enhancing, and filtering.

- We'll look at how we can fiddle with the individual bits that make up an integer value.

- We'll also see how we work with Unicode characters and how characters are encoded into bytes.

- Learning to work with Unicode characters will allow us to encode data in the pixels of an image file. We'll look at the two common steganography algorithms.

- We'll also take a quick side trip to look at secure hashes. This will show us how to make messages that can't be altered in transmission.

Python is a very powerful programming language. In this chapter, we'll see a lot of sophistication available. We'll also lay a foundation to look at web services and geocoding in the next chapter.

Background briefing – handling file formats

As we've observed so far, our data comes in a wide variety of physical formats. In *Chapter 1, Our Espionage Toolkit*, we looked at ZIP files, which are archives that contain other files. In *Chapter 2, Acquiring Intelligence Data*, we looked at JSON files, which serialize many kinds of Python objects.

In this chapter, we're going to review some previous technology and then look at working specifically with CSV files. The important part is to look at the various kinds of image files that we might need to work with.

In all cases, Python encourages looking at a file as a kind of context. This means that we should strive to open files using the `with` statement so that we can be sure the file is properly closed when we're done with the processing. This doesn't always work out perfectly, so there are some exceptions.

Working with the OS filesystem

There are many modules for working with files. We'll focus on two: `glob` and `os`.

glob

The `glob` module implements filesystem *globbing* rules. When we use `*.jpg` in a command at the terminal prompt, a standard OS shell tool will *glob* or expand the wildcard name into a matching list of actual file names, as shown in the following snippet:

```
MacBookPro-SLott:code slott$ ls *.jpg
1drachmi_1973.jpg        IPhone_Internals.jpg
Common_face_of_one_euro_coin.jpg  LHD_warship.jpg
```

The POSIX standard is for `*.jpg` to be expanded by the shell, prior to the `ls` program being run. In Windows, this is not always the case.

The Python `glob` module contains the `glob()` function that does this job from within a Python program. Here's an example:

```
>>> import glob
>>> glob.glob("*.jpg")
```

```
['1drachmi_1973.jpg', 'Common_face_of_one_euro_coin.jpg', 'IPhone_
Internals.jpg', 'LHD_warship.jpg']
```

When we evaluated `glob.glob("*.jpg")`, the return value was a list of strings with the names of matching files.

os

Many files have a `path/name.extension` format. For Windows, a device prefix and the backslash is used (`c:path\name.ext`). The Python `os` package provides a `path` module with a number of functions for working with file names and paths irrespective of any vagaries of punctuation. As the `path` module is in the `os` package, the components will have two levels of namespace containers: `os.path`.

We must always use functions from the `os.path` module for working with filenames. There are numerous functions to split paths, join paths, and create absolute paths from relative paths. For example, we should use `os.path.splitext()` to separate a filename from the extension. Here's an example:

```
>>> import os
>>> os.path.splitext( "1drachmi_1973.jpg" )
('1drachmi_1973', '.jpg')
```

We've separated the filename from the extension without writing any of our own code. There's no reason to write our own parsers when the standard library already has them written.

Processing simple text files

In some cases, our files contain ordinary text. In this case, we can open the file and process the lines as follows:

```
with open("some_file") as data:
    for line in data:
        ... process the line ...
```

This is the most common way to work with text files. Each line processed by the `for` loop will include a trailing \n character.

We can use a simple generator expression to strip the trailing spaces from each line:

```
with open("some_file") as data:
    for line in (raw.rstrip() for raw in data):
        ... process the line ...
```

We've inserted a generator expression into the `for` statement. The generator expression has three parts: a subexpression (`raw.rstrip()`), a target variable (`raw`), and a source iterable collection (`data`). Each line in the source iterable, `data`, is assigned to the target, `raw`, and the subexpression is evaluated. Each result from the generator expression is made available to the outer `for` loop.

We can visually separate the generator expression into a separate line of code:

```
with open("some_file") as data:
    clean_lines = (raw.rstrip() for raw in data)
    for line in clean_lines:
        ... process the line ...
```

We wrote the generator expression outside the `for` statement. We assigned the generator — not the resulting collection — to the `clean_lines` variable to clarify its purpose. A generator doesn't generate any output until the individual lines are required by another iterator, in this case, the `for` loop. There's no real overhead: the processing is simply separated visually.

This technique allows us to separate different design considerations. We can separate the text cleanup from the important processing inside the `for` statement.

We can expand on the cleanup by writing additional generators:

```
with open("some_file") as data:
    clean_lines = (raw.rstrip() for raw in data)
    non_blank_lines = (line for line in clean_lines if len(line) != 0)
    for line in non_blank_lines:
        ... process the line ...
```

We've broken down two preprocessing steps into two separate generator expressions. The first expression removes the `\n` character from the end of each line. The second generator expression uses the optional `if` clause — it will get lines from the first generator expression and only pass lines if the length is not 0. This is a filter that rejects blank lines. The final `for` statement only gets nonblank lines that have had the `\n` character removed.

Working with ZIP files

A ZIP archive contains one or more files. To use `with` with ZIP archives, we need to import the `zipfile` module:

```
import zipfile
```

Generally, we can open an archive using something like the following:

```
with zipfile.ZipFile("demo.zip", "r") as archive:
```

This creates a context so that we can work with the file and be sure that it's properly closed at the end of the indented context.

When we want to create an archive, we can provide an additional parameter:

```
with ZipFile("test.zip", "w", compression=zipfile.zipfile.ZIP_
DEFLATED) as archive:
```

This will create a ZIP file that uses a simple compression algorithm to save space. If we're reading members of a ZIP archive, we can use a nested context to open this member file, as shown in the following snippet:

```
with archive.open("some_file") as member:
    ...process member...
```

As we showed in *Chapter 1, Our Espionage Toolkit*, once we've opened a member for reading, it's similar to an ordinary OS file. The nested context allows us to use ordinary file processing operations on the member. We used the following example earlier:

```
import zipfile
with zipfile.ZipFile( "demo.zip", "r" ) as archive:
    archive.printdir()
    first = archive.infolist()[0]
    with archive.open(first) as member:
        text= member.read()
        print( text )
```

We used a context to open the archive. We used a nested context to open a member of the archive. Not all files can be read this way. Members that are images, for example, can't be read directly by Pillow; they must be extracted to a temporary file. We'd do something like this:

```
import zipfile
with zipfile.ZipFile( "photos.zip", "r" ) as archive:
    archive.extract("warship.png")
```

This will extract a member named `warship.png` from the archive and create a local file. Pillow can then work with the extracted file.

Working with JSON files

A JSON file contains a Python object that's been serialized in JSON notation. To work with JSON files, we need to import the `json` module:

```
import json
```

The file processing context doesn't really apply well to JSON files. We don't generally have the file open for any extended time when processing it. Often, the `with` statement context is just one line of code. We might create a file like this:

```
...create an_object...
with open("some_file.json", "w") as output:
    json.save(an_object, output)
```

This is all that's required to create a JSON-encoded file. Often, we'll contrive to make the object we're serializing a list or a dict so that we can save multiple objects in a single file. To retrieve the object, we generally do something that's similarly simple, as shown in the following code:

```
with open("some_file.json") as input:
    an_object= json.load(input)
...process an_object...
```

This will decode the object and save it in the given variable. If the file contains a list, we can iterate through the object to process each item in the list. If the file contains a dictionary, we might work with specific key values of this dictionary.

 The processing applied to the resulting object, `an_object`, is outside the context of the `with` statement.

Once the Python object has been created, we no longer need the file context. The resources associated with the file can be released, and we can focus our processing steps on the resulting object.

Working with CSV files

CSV stands for **comma-separated values**. While one of the most common CSV formats uses the quote character and commas, the CSV idea is readily applicable to any file that has a column-separator character. We might have a file with each data item separated by tab characters, written as `\t` in Python. This is also a kind of CSV file that uses the tab character to fill the role of a comma.

We'll use the `csv` module to process these files:

```
import csv
```

When we open a CSV file, we must create a *reader* or *writer* that parses the various rows of data in the file. Let's say we downloaded the historical record of bitcoin prices. You can download this data from `https://coinbase.com/api/doc/1.0/prices/historical.html`. See *Chapter 2, Acquiring Intelligence Data*, for more information.

The data is in the CSV notation. Once we've read the string, we need to create a CSV reader around the data. As the data was just read into a big string variable, we don't need to use the filesystem. We can use in-memory processing to create a file-like object, as shown in the following code:

```
import io
with urllib.request.urlopen( query_history ) as document:
    history_data= document.read().decode("utf-8")
reader= csv.reader( io.StringIO(history_data) )
```

We've used the `urllib.request.urlopen()` function to make a GET request to the given URL. The response will be in bytes. We decoded the characters from these bytes and saved them in a variable named `history_data`.

In order to make this amenable to the `csv.Reader` class, we used the `io.StringIO` class to wrap the data. This creates a file-like object without actually wasting time to create a file on the disk somewhere.

We can now read individual rows from the `reader` object, as shown in the following code:

```
for row in reader:
    print( row )
```

This `for` loop will step through each row of the CSV file. The various columns of data will be separated; each row will be a tuple of individual column values.

If we have *tab-separated* data, we'd modify the reader by providing additional details about the file format. We might, for example, use `rdr= csv.reader(some_file, delimiter='\t')` to specify that there are tab-separated values instead of comma-separated ones.

JPEG and PNG graphics – pixels and metadata

An image is composed of picture elements called pixels. Each pixel is a dot. For computer displays, the individual dots are encoded using **red-green-blue** (**RGB**) colors. Each displayed pixel is a sum of the levels of red, green, and blue light. For printing, the colors might be switched to **cyan-magenta-yellow-key** (**CMYK**) colors.

An image file contains an encoding of the various pixels of the image. The image file may also contain metadata about the image. The metadata information is sometimes called **tags** and even **Exif tags**.

An image file can use a variety of encodings for each pixel. A pure black and white image only needs 1 bit for each pixel. High-quality photographs may use one byte for each color, leading to 24 bits per pixel. In some cases, we might add a transparency mask or look for even higher-resolution color. This leads to four bytes per pixel.

The issue rapidly turns into a question of the amount of storage required. A picture that fills an iPhone display has 326 pixels per inch. The display has 1136 by 640 pixels. If each pixel uses 4 bytes of color information, then the image involves 3 MB of memory.

Consider a scanned image that's of 8 1/2" by 11" at 326 pixels per inch The image is 2762 x 3586 pixels, a total of 39 MB. Some scanners are capable of producing images at 1200 pixels per inch: that file would be of 673 MB.

Different image files reflect different strategies to compress this immense amount of data without losing the quality of the image.

A naive compression algorithm can make the files somewhat smaller. TIFF files, for example, use a fairly simple compression. The algorithms used by JPEG, however, are quite sophisticated and lead to relatively small file sizes while retaining much—but not all—of the original image. While JPEG is very good at compressing, the compressed image is not perfect—details are lost to achieve good compression. This makes JPEG weak for steganography where we'll be tweaking the bits to conceal a message in an image.

We can call JPEG compression lossy because some bits can be lost. We can call TIFF compression lossless because all the original bits can be recovered. Once bits are lost, they can't be recovered. As our message will only be tweaking a few bits, JPEG compression can corrupt our hidden message.

When we work with images in Pillow, it will be similar to working with a JSON file. We'll open and load the image. We can then process the object in our program. When we're done, we'll save the modified image.

Using the Pillow library

We're going to add some cool Python software to process images. The Pillow package is a sophisticated image-processing library. This library provides extensive file format support, an efficient internal representation, and fairly powerful image processing capabilities. For more information, visit `https://pypi.python.org/pypi/Pillow/2.1.0`. The Pillow documentation will provide important background in what needs to be done. The installation guide on the PyPi web page is essential reading, you will get some additional details here. The core Pillow documentation is at `http://pillow.readthedocs.org/en/latest/`.

Note that Pillow will install a package named `PIL`. This assures that Pillow (the project) creates a module that's compatible with the **Python Imaging Library** (**PIL**). We'll be importing modules from the `PIL` package, even though we'll be installing software created by the Pillow project.

Adding the required supporting libraries

If you're a Windows agent, then you can skip this section. The folks who build Pillow have you firmly in mind. For everyone else, your OS may not be Pillow ready.

Before installing Pillow, some supporting software infrastructure must be in place. Once all the supporting software is ready, then Pillow can be installed.

GNU/Linux secrets

We need to have the following libraries in our GNU/Linux configuration. Odds are good that these files are already present in a given distribution. If these files aren't present, it's time to perform some upgrades or installations. Install the following:

- **libjpeg**: This library provides access to JPEG images; versions 6b, 8, and 9 have been tested
- **zlib**: This library provides access to compressed PNG images
- **libtiff**: This library provides access to TIFF images; versions 3.x and 4.0 have been tested
- **libfreetype**: This library provides type-related services
- **littlecms**: This library provides color management
- **libwebp**: This library provides access to the WebP format

Each Linux distribution has a unique approach to installing and configuring the libraries. We can't cover them all.

Once the supporting libraries are in place, we can use the `easy_install-3.3 pillow` command. We'll review this in the *Installing and confirming Pillow* section.

Mac OS X secrets

To install Pillow on a Mac, we require three preliminary steps to be performed. We'll need Xcode and homebrew, then we'll use homebrew.

To get Xcode for Mac OS X, visit `https://developer.apple.com/xcode/downloads/`. Every Mac OS X agent should have Xcode, even if they're not going to write native Mac OS X or iOS apps.

When installing Xcode, we must be sure that we also install the command-line developer tools. This is another big download above and beyond the basic XCode download.

Once we have Xcode command-line tools, the second preliminary step is to install Homebrew from `http://brew.sh`. This application builds and installs GNU/Linux binaries for Mac OS X. Homebrew is not directly related to Python; this is a popular Mac OS X developer tool.

The Homebrew installation is a single line entered in the terminal window:

```
ruby -e "$(curl -fsSL https://raw.github.com/Homebrew/homebrew/go/
install)"
```

This will use the curl program to download the Homebrew installation kit from GitHub. It will use Ruby to run this installation program, building the various Homebrew tools and scripts. The Homebrew installation suggests using `brew doctor` to check the development environment. There may be some cleanup to do before proceeding.

The third step is to use the `brew` program to install the required additional libraries for Pillow. This command line will handle that:

```
brew install libtiff libjpeg webp littlecms
```

Periodically, we may need to upgrade the libraries Homebrew knows about. The command is simply `brew update`. We may also need to upgrade the various packages we installed. This is done using `brew upgrade libtiff libjpeg webp littlecms`.

When we've finished the three preliminary steps, we can use the `easy_install-3.3 pillow` command. We'll review this in the *Installing and confirming pillow* section.

Windows secrets

The Pillow distribution for Windows contains all the various libraries prebuilt. The kit will have the following already installed:

- **libjpeg**
- **zlib**
- **libtiff**
- **libfreetype**
- **littlecms**
- **libwebp**

After the installation is complete, these modules will all be present and used by Pillow.

Installing and confirming Pillow

Once all the required supporting tools are in place (or you're a Windows agent), the next step is to install Pillow.

This should amount to the following command:

```
sudo easy_install-3.3 pillow
```

Windows agents must omit the `sudo` command that prefixes the `easy_install` command.

Part of the output will look something like this (details will vary):

```
--------------------------------------------------------------------
PIL SETUP SUMMARY
--------------------------------------------------------------------
version         Pillow 2.4.0
platform        darwin 3.3.4 (v3.3.4:7ff62415e426, Feb  9 2014, 00:29:34)
                [GCC 4.2.1 (Apple Inc. build 5666) (dot 3)]
--------------------------------------------------------------------
--- TKINTER support available
--- JPEG support available
*** OPENJPEG (JPEG2000) support not available
--- ZLIB (PNG/ZIP) support available
--- LIBTIFF support available
```

```
*** FREETYPE2 support not available
*** LITTLECMS2 support not available
--- WEBP support available
--- WEBPMUX support available
--------------------------------------------------------------------
To add a missing option, make sure you have the required
library, and set the corresponding ROOT variable in the
setup.py script.

To check the build, run the selftest.py script.
```

This tells us that some libraries were not available, and we can't do every kind of processing. If we don't intend to work with JPEG2000 files or do complex color management, this is acceptable. On the other hand, if we think we're going to do more complex processing, we may need to track down additional modules and redo our Pillow installation.

The Pillow installation creates PIL. The top-level package will be named `PIL`.

We can test Pillow using it's own internal test script, `PIL.selftest`. Otherwise, we can use it like this:

```
>>> from PIL import Image
```

If this works, then the PIL package is installed. We can then open an image file to see whether things are working properly. The following code shows us that PIL happily opened an image file for us:

```
>>> pix= Image.open("1drachmi_1973.jpg")
>>> pix
<PIL.JpegImagePlugin.JpegImageFile image mode=RGB size=198x194 at
0x10183BA90>
```

This shows us that PIL was able to save the file in a different format:

```
>>> pix.save("test.tiff")
```

This simple-looking step requires Pillow do a tremendous amount of computation to convert from one format to another.

Decoding and encoding image data

Image files are encoded in a form that makes them handy for reading and writing, but not so useful for detailed processing. We'll need to decode an image from the file format to a useful internal representation. Pillow greatly simplifies the processes of decoding and encoding image files. Our general strategy for working with an image file is to start with the following recipe:

```
from PIL import Image
pix= Image.open("LHD_warship.jpg")
```

Pillow extracts a number of interesting attributes from the image metadata. There's a complex hierarchy of additional information that comes along with the image. We'll review some of this metadata in detail.

At the top level, there are some pieces of information that describe some details of the encoding. These are available in a dictionary that is the `info` attribute of the `pix` object we created. We can use the `keys()` method of a dictionary to see what's present in the metadata, as shown in the following snippet:

```
>>> pix.info.keys()
dict_keys(['jfif_density', 'icc_profile', 'jfif_version', 'jfif',
'exif', 'jfif_unit', 'dpi'])
```

Of these keys, the value mapped to the `exif` key is often the most interesting. This is the exchangeable image file format data that provides additional details about the image. The other items are technical details about the image encoding.

The Exif data isn't automatically decoded by Pillow. We need to use the `_getexif()` method to see what's in the `exif` key for the image. Note the leading `_` sign to this name. This is atypical. This method will give us a dictionary of tags and values. Here's an example:

```
>>> exif= pix._getexif()
>>> exif.keys()
dict_keys([36864, 37121, 37378, 36867, 36868, 41989, 40960, 37383,
37385, 37386, 40962, 271, 272, 37521, 37522, 40963, 37396, 41495,
41988, 282, 283, 33434, 37500, 34850, 40961, 34853, 41986, 34855, 296,
34665, 41987, 41990, 42034, 33437, 305, 306, 42035, 42036, 41729])
```

This doesn't look too useful. The good news is that the numeric codes are defined in a separate module. We can use a dictionary lookup to translate numeric codes to words. Here's an example:

```
>>> import PIL.ExifTags
>>> for k, v in pix._getexif().items():
...     print( PIL.ExifTags.TAGS[k], v )
```

This will iterate through the Exif tags and values, translating the tag values to words. Now we can find the useful identifying information about the image. The output shows us details like these:

```
Software 7.1.1
DateTime 2014:05:10 09:59:22
LensMake Apple
LensModel iPhone 4 back camera 3.85mm f/2.8
```

Of these Exif tags, the number 34853, the GPSInfo tag form a subdictionary with yet more cryptic numeric keys. This secondary set of numeric codes are defined by the PIL.ExifTags.GPSTAGS mapping.

This leads us to something like the following to dump the information for an image:

```
img= Image.open(name)
print( name, img.format, img.mode, img.size )
for key in img.info:
    if key == 'exif':
        for k,v in img._getexif().items():
            if k == 34853: # GPSInfo
                print( " ", PIL.ExifTags.TAGS[k], v )
                for gk, gv in v.items():
                    print( "  ", PIL.ExifTags.GPSTAGS[gk], gv )
            else:
                print( " ", PIL.ExifTags.TAGS[k], v )
    elif key == 'icc_profile':
        print( key ) # Skip these details
    else:
        print( key, img.info[key] )
```

This will iterate through the top-level .info dictionary associated with the image. Within this top-level .info dictionary, if the key is exif, we'll iterate through the Exif dictionary items. Within the Exif dictionary, we'll translate the numeric keys to meaningful strings. If we find the key, 34853 (GPSInfo), we know that we have another dictionary that is more deeply nested. We'll use another nested for loop to iterate through the items of the GPSInfo dictionary, translating those keys to useful strings.

We might see this kind of output.

```
Common_face_of_one_euro_coin.jpg JPEG RGB (320, 312)
  ExifOffset 26
  ExifImageWidth 320
  ExifImageHeight 312
jfif_version (1, 1)
```

```
jfif_unit 0
jfif_density (1, 1)
jfif 257
```

In this output, the Exif data isn't too interesting. The other details don't seem useful either.

When we look at a picture that's richly detailed with metadata, there might be over 30 individual pieces of Exif data. For example, here's a section of some Exif data found in one image:

```
DateTimeOriginal 2009:03:18 04:24:24
DateTimeDigitized 2009:03:18 04:24:24
SceneCaptureType 0
MeteringMode 3
Flash 16
FocalLength (20, 1)
ApertureValue (35, 8)
FocalPlaneXResolution (257877, 53)
Make Canon
Model Canon EOS DIGITAL REBEL XSi
```

This can tell someone a lot about how the picture was taken.

When we have pictures taken with modern cameras (such as phone cameras) with GPS data, some additional information is packed into the Exif. For some cameras, we'll find this kind of information as follows:

```
GPSLatitudeRef N
GPSLatitude ((36, 1), (50, 1), (4012, 100))
GPSLongitudeRef W
GPSLongitude ((76, 1), (17, 1), (3521, 100))
```

The GPS coordinates from the camera are a little odd looking. We can turn each of these tuple-of-tuples structures into numbers such as 36°50'40.12"N and 76°17'35.21"W. Once we have the location, we can figure out where the picture was taken.

A quick check on the nautical chart 12253 shows that the picture was taken from a dock in Norfolk, Virginia. *Every secret agent has a set of nautical charts, right? If not, visit* `http://www.nauticalcharts.noaa.gov/mcd/Raster/`.

The ICC profile shows the details of color and rendering for the image. For details on the data encoded here, see the applicable specifications from `http://www.color.org/specification/ICC1v43_2010-12.pdf`. It's not clear that this information is very helpful for what we're doing.

What's more helpful is looking at the picture. LHD 3 painted on the hull seems to be important.

Manipulating images – resizing and thumbnails

The Pillow software allows us to perform a number of manipulations on the image. We can, without too much additional work, resize, crop, rotate, or apply any number of filters to an image.

The most important reason for using PIL is that we have a reproducible, automated process. We can find many kinds of manual image manipulation software. The problem with these desktop tools is that a manual sequence of steps is irreproducible. The benefit of using Pillow for this manipulation is we know precisely what we did.

One common resizing is to create a thumbnail image from a larger image. Here's how we can create useful thumbnail versions of a collection of images:

```python
from PIL import Image
import glob
import os

for filename in glob.glob("*.jpg"):
    name, ext = os.path.splitext( filename )
    if name.endswith("_thumb"):
        continue
    img = Image.open( filename )
    thumb= img.copy()
    w, h = img.size
    largest = max(w,h)
    w_n, h_n = w*128//largest, h*128//largest
    print( "Resize", filename, "from", w,h, "to", w_n,h_n )
    thumb.thumbnail( (w_n, h_n), PIL.Image.ANTIALIAS )
    thumb.save( name+"_thumb"+ext )
```

We've imported the modules we need: `PIL.Image`, `glob` and `os`. We used `glob.glob("*.jpg")` to locate all of the JPEG files in the current working directory. We used `os.path.splitext()` to tease apart the base filename and extension. If the filename already ends in `_thumb`, we'll continue the `for` loop. No more processing will happen for this filename; the `for` statement will advance to the next item in the glob sequence.

We opened the image file and immediately created a copy. This allows us to work with the original image, if we need to, as well as work with the copy.

We've extracted the size of the original image and assigned each item of the tuples to two separate variables, w and h. We picked the largest of the two dimensions using the max() function. If the picture was in the landscape mode, the width will be largest; if the picture was in the portrait mode, the height will be largest.

We've computed the size of the thumbnail image, w_t and h_t. The pair of calculations will assure that the largest dimension is limited to 128 pixels and the smaller dimension will be scaled proportionally.

We used the thumbnail() method of the thumb object, which is a copy of the original image. We provided a two-tuple with the new dimensions. It's essential that we include () around (w_n, h_n) to create a tuple for the first argument value to the thumbnail() method. We also provided the resample function to use; in this case, we used the PIL.Image.ANTIALIAS function, as this produces good (but slow) results.

Here's the thumbnail of our LHD warship:

The image is pretty small. This makes it good for attaching it to an e-mail. However, for more serious intelligence work, we'll need to blow it up, crop it, and enhance it.

Manipulating images – cropping

When we look at our LHD warship image, we notice that the ship number is almost visible on the bow. We'd like to crop that portion of the image and perhaps, blow it up. Cropping without a visual editor involves a certain amount of hit-or-miss processing.

Even from the command line, we can crop an image interactively by using the `show()` method of an image, as shown in the following code:

```
>>> from PIL import Image
>>> ship= Image.open( "LHD_warship.jpg" )
>>> ship.size
(2592, 1936)
```

We can try different bounding boxes until we locate the logo. One way to start is to break the image into thirds in each direction; this leads to nine sections, computed via relatively simple rules as follows:

```
>>> w, h = ship.size
>>> ship.crop( box=(w//3,0,2*w//3,h//3) ).show()
>>> ship.crop( box=(w//3,h//3,2*w//3,2*h//3) ).show()
```

The bounding box for a crop operation requires a four-tuple with the left, top, right, and bottom sides, in that order. The values must be integers and the `()` brackets are required to create four-tuple, instead of four separate argument values. The horizontal dividing lines are at 0, $w//3$, $2*w//3$, and w. The vertical dividing lines are at 0, $h//3$, $2*h//3$, and h. We can use various combinations to locate the various sections of the image and show each section.

Entering formulae like this is error prone. It's much nicer to work with a bounding box defined by a top-left coordinate pair. We can fiddle in a width and compute the height to maintain the picture's proportions. If we use something like the following, we only have to tweak the x and y coordinates:

```
>>> p=h/w
>>> x,y=3*w//12, 3*h//12
>>> ship.crop( box=(x,y,x+600,int(y+600*p)) ).show()
>>> x,y=3*w//12, 5*h//12
>>> ship.crop( box=(x,y,x+600,int(y+600*p)) ).show()
```

We can fiddle with the x and y values. Then we can use the up arrow key to fetch the `ship.crop().show()` line back again. This allows us to step through the image manually, just changing x and y.

We can do a little better at generalizing the bounding boxes of image sections. Consider this list of fractions:

```
>>> from fractions import Fraction
>>> slices = 6
>>> box = [ Fraction(i,slices) for i in range(slices+1) ]
>>> box
[Fraction(0, 1), Fraction(1, 6), Fraction(1, 3), Fraction(1, 2),
Fraction(2, 3), Fraction(5, 6), Fraction(1, 1)]
```

We have defined the number of slices we want to make. In this case, we'll divide the image into 1/6, giving us 36 individual boxes. We then computed the `slice+1` lines at positions between $w \times \frac{0}{6}$ and $w \times \frac{6}{6}$. Here is an illustration that shows the slicing of the image into a 6 x 6 grid. Each cell has a boundary defined by the `box` sequence:

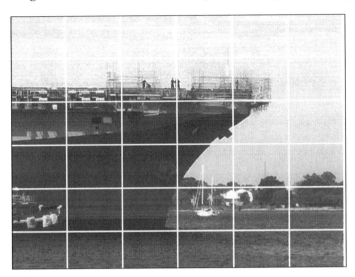

This uses the following pair of nested `for` loops with the `box` fractions to generate the individual boundaries for various pieces of the image:

```
for i in range(slices):
    for j in range(slices):
        bounds = int(w*box[i]), int(h*box[j]), int(w*box[i+1]),
int(h*box[j+1])
```

Each boundary box has the left, top, right, and bottom side as a four-tuple. We've picked values of two variables to enumerate all 36 combinations from (0,0) to (5,5). We've picked two adjacent values from our list of fractions, `lines`. This will give us all 36 bounding boxes from top-left to bottom-right.

We can then crop our original image using each of these definitions of box and show all 36 slices, looking for the one that's closest to the subject matter we're looking for. Also, we might want to resize each image and make it twice as big.

We can use the following to show each box:

```
print( bounds )
ship.crop( bounds ).show()
```

This will display the original image cropped to each of the slices. The `bounds` object is a four-tuple with the boundary information.

We can slightly optimize the expression that computes the bounds using the map() function:

```
bounds = map( int, (w*box[i], h*box[j], w*box[i+1], h*box[j+1]) )
```

The map() function will apply a function to each element of the associated collection. In this example, we apply the int() function to each value of the bounding box. It turns out that this is the image we want:

```
slices = 12
box = [ Fraction(i,slices) for i in range(slices+1) ]
bounds = map( int, (w*box[3], h*box[6], w*box[5], h*box[7]) )
logo= ship.crop( bounds )
logo.show()
logo.save( "LHD_number.jpg" )
```

We've cropped the image using two adjacent boxes. The boxes at (3,6) and (4,6) incorporate the ship's identification number nicely. We created a single four-tuple with the combined bounding box and cropped the original image to pick up just the logo. We used the show() method of the logo object, which will pop up an image viewer. We also saved it so that we'd have a file we could work with later.

We might want to resize the cropped image. We can use code like this to blow up the image:

```
w,h= logo.size
logo.resize( (w*3,h*3) )
```

This will use the original size as a basis so that the expanded image retains the original proportions. As with other operations, the size is given as a tuple and the inner () brackets are required to define a tuple. Without the inner () brackets, these would be two separate argument values.

Here's the cropped image:

That's kind of murky and hard to work with. We'll need to enhance it.

Manipulating images – enhancing

The original picture is pretty grainy. We'd like to enhance the details of the slice we found. Pillow has a number of filters than can help modify an image. Unlike popular TV shows and movies, there's no enhance feature that magically makes a poor image spectacular.

We can modify an image, and sometimes, it's more usable. We can also modify an image and leave it no better than we found it. The third choice—not often available to secret agents—is that we might make the results more artistic than the original image.

We have three modules in the Pillow package that contain filter-like processing:

- `ImageEnhance`
- `ImageFilter`
- `ImageOps`

The `ImageEnhance` module contains `enhance` class definitions. We create an enhancer object by binding an enhancer and an image. We then use that bound object to create enhanced versions of a given image. An enhancer allows us to make many incremental changes to an image. We can think of these as simple knobs, which might be turned to tweak the image.

The `ImageFilter` module contains filters functions that will revise the image, creating a new image object that we might save. These various kinds of filter objects are plugged into the image's `filter()` method. A filter can be imagined as a way to reduce the volume of information in the image; the image is usually simpler after being filtered.

The `ImageOps` module contains functions that transform one image to create a new image. These are different from filtering and enhancing. They're not necessarily reducing the data nor are they simple knobs to tweak an image. The `ImageOps` module tends to perform more complex transformations.

We'll start out with some simple enhancers in the `PIL.ImageEnhance` module, specifically, the `Contrast` class. We won't present each individual class; the more systematic exploration is for field agents.

We'll start with one of the four enhancers: the `Contrast` class. Here's how we can use it:

```
>>> from PIL import ImageEnhance
>>> e= ImageEnhance.Contrast(logo)
>>> e.enhance(2.0).show()
>>> e.enhance(4.0).show()
>>> e.enhance(8.0).show()
```

This builds an enhancer, based on the specific algorithm and the image we're working with. We've assigned this enhancer to the e variable. We then performed an enhance operation with a specific parameter value and showed the resulting image.

The last image is pretty nice. We can save a copy of this image with `e.enhance(8.0).save( "LHD_Number_1.jpg" )`.

Here's how the logo looks with the Contrast enhancement set to 8:

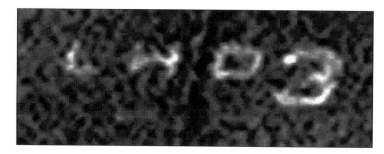

Someone might be able to work with this image. As a field agent, you'll need to experiment with the other three enhancement filters: color, brightness, and sharpness. You might be able to extract even more detail from the image.

This is the first step in defining a reproducible, automated process. Using Python from the command line means that we have a record of precisely what we did. We can reduce the process to an automated script.

Manipulating images – filtering

We've looked at the ImageEnhance module to improve an image. We can also filter via the image's filter() method. The ImageFilter module defines 18 different filters. When we use a filter, we'll provide the filter object to the Image.filter() method.

We'll pick just one of these filters. The ImageFilter.EDGE_ENHANCE module seems to be helpful for distinguishing between the light-colored letter and the dark-colored background. Emphasizing on the transition in color might make the letters more visible.

Here's an example of using the ImageFilter.EDGE_ENHANCE filter in the filter() method of an image:

```
>>> from PIL import ImageFilter
>>> logo.filter( ImageFilter.EDGE_ENHANCE ).show()
```

We've used the filter method to create and show a new image.

While this is good, it seems like our enhancement attempts might work better with the `ImageEnhance.Contrast` class we used earlier. Here's how we can apply a sequence of transformations.

The following code applies the specific filter to the image and creates a new image:

```
>>> e.enhance(8.0).filter( ImageFilter.EDGE_ENHANCE ).save( "LHD_
Number_2.jpg" )
```

We've created an enhanced image and then applied a filter to it. This creates something even more crisp and possibly more usable than the original image.

This is our filtered and enhanced image:

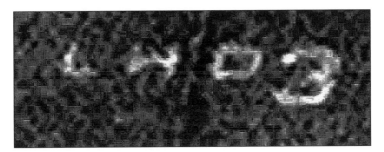

The filter has made some minor changes to the previously saved image. The edge on the lower loop of 3 might be a bit more crisp. We'll need to change some more things.

Some filters (such as the `EDGE_ENHANCE` object) have no parameters or options. Other filters have parameters that can be applied to change the way they work. For example, the `ModeFilter()` will reduce a given section of the image to the most common color value within that section; we provide a parameter for the number of pixels to consider when computing the mode.

Here's an example of combining several operations to create a new image:

```
>>> p1= e.enhance(8.0).filter( ImageFilter.ModeFilter(8) )
>>> p1.filter( ImageFilter.EDGE_ENHANCE ).show()
```

This seems to be tending towards art and away from proper intelligence gathering. However, a good field agent will work with some additional filters and filter parameters to look for better enhancement techniques.

Manipulating images – ImageOps

We've looked at the `ImageEnhance` module to improve an image. We've also looked at a few other filters in the `ImageFilter` module. The `ImageOps` module provides 13 additional transformations that we can use to improve our image.

We'll look at the `ImageOps.autocontrast()` function, as shown in the following snippet. This will adjust the various pixels so that the brightness levels fill the entire 8-bit space from 0 to 255. An image that's dark or washed out lacks contrast, and the pixels are all piled up at the dark end or the bright end of the spectrum.

```
>>> from PIL import ImageOps
>>> ImageOps.autocontrast( logo ).show()
>>> logo.show()
```

This shows an image with `autocontrast` applied and the original image. This shows the striking difference between the original clipping and an image that uses the full range from dark to light. That seems to be just what HQ would want.

Let's tweak the contrast a little further to really make the numbers stand out:

```
>>> ac= ImageEnhance.Contrast( ImageOps.autocontrast( logo ) )
>>> ac.enhance( 2.5 ).save( "LHD_Number_3.jpg" )
```

This seems to be the most startling enhancement we can do:

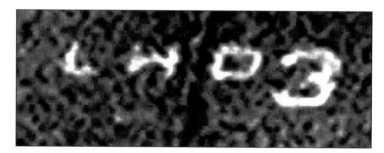

This might be good enough. A competent field agent should play with the rest of the `ImageOps` transformations to see whether more improvement is possible.

At this point, we have the outline for a reproducible, automated process. We know precisely what we did to enhance the image. We can use our series of experiments to create an automated script for image enhancement.

Some approaches to steganography

There are many more things we can do with image files. One thing we can do is use steganography to conceal messages inside image files. As image files are large, complex, and relatively noisy, adding a few extra bits of data won't make much of a visible change to the image or the file.

Sometimes this is summarized as adding a **digital watermark** to an image. We're going to subtly alter the image in a way that we can recognize and recover it later.

Adding a message can be seen as a lossy modification to the image. Some of the original pixels will be unrecoverable. As the JPEG compression, in general, already involves minor losses, tweaking the image as part of steganography will be a similar level of image corruption.

Speaking of losses, the JPEG format can, and will, tweak some of the bits in our image. Consequently, it's difficult to perform steganography with JPEG. Rather than wrestle with JPEG details, we'll use the TIFF format for our concealed messages.

There are two common approaches to concealing a message in an image:

- **Using a color channel**: If we overwrite some bytes in just one color channel, we'll be shifting a part of the color of a few pixels in the area we overwrote. It will only be a few of millions of pixels, and it will only be one of the three (or four) colors. If we confine the tweaking to the edge, it's not too noticeable.

- **Using the least significant bits (LSBs) of each byte**: If we overwrite the least significant bit in a series of bytes, we'll make an extremely minor shift in the image. We have to limit the size of our message because we can only encode one byte per pixel. A small picture that's $432 * 161 = 69,552$ pixels can encode 8,694 bytes of data. If we use the UTF-8 encoding for our characters, we should be able to cram an 8 K message into that image. If we use UTF-16, we'd only get a 4 K message. This technique works even for grayscale images where there's only one channel.

In addition to the JPEG compression problem, there are some color encoding schemes that don't work out well with either of these steganography approaches. The modes, known as **P**, **I**, and **F**, present a bit of a problem. These color modes involve mapping a color code to a palette. In these cases, the byte is not the level of gray or the level of a color; when using a palette, the bytes are a reference to a color. Making a 1-bit change might lead to a profound change in the color selected from the underlying palette. The color 5 might be a pleasant sea-foam green, the color 4 might be an awful magenta. A 1-bit change between 5 and 4 may be a noticeable out-of-place dot.

For our purposes, we can switch the source image to RGB (or CMYK) before applying our steganography encoding. The basic change to the color mode might be visible to someone who had access to the original image. However, the hidden message will remain obscured unless they also know our steganography algorithm.

Our strategy works like this:

1. Get the bytes from the pixels of the image.
2. Transform our secret message from a Unicode string into a sequence of bits.
3. For each bit of our secret message, adulterate 1 byte of the original image. As we're tweaking the least significant bit, one of two things will happen.

    ° We'll make an image pixel value into an even number to encode a 0 bit from our secret message

    ° We'll make an image pixel value into an odd number to encode a 1 bit from our secret message

We'll work with two parallel sequences of values:

- The bytes from the image (ideally enough to encode our entire message)
- The bits from our secret message

The idea is to step through each byte of the image and incorporate 1 bit of the secret message into that image byte. The cool feature of this is that some pixel values might not need to actually change. If we're encoding a byte in a pixel that's already odd, we won't change the image at all.

This means that we need to perform the following important steps:

- Get the bytes in the red channel of the image
- Get the bytes from a Unicode message
- Get the bits from the message bytes
- Tweak the image pixel byte using a message bit, and update the image

We'll tackle these one at a time, then we'll weld it all together at the end.

Getting the red-channel data

Let's look at encoding our message in an image using the red channel LSB encoding. Why red? Why not? Men may have some degree of red-green color blindness; if they're less likely to see a shift in this channel, then we've further concealed our image from a few prying eyes.

The first question is this: how do we tinker with the bytes of the original image?

The PIL `Image` object has the `getpixel()` and `putpixel()` methods that allow us to get the various color band values.

We can peel out individual pixels from the image like this:

```
>>> y = 0
>>> for x in range(64):
...     print(ship.getpixel( (x,y) ))
...
(234, 244, 243)
(234, 244, 243)
(233, 243, 242)
(233, 243, 242)
etc.
```

We've provided an `(x,y)` two-tuple to the `getpixel()` method. This shows us that each pixel in the image is a three-tuple. It's not obvious what the three numbers are. We can use `ship.getbands()` to get this information, as shown in the following snippet:

```
>>> ship.getbands()
('R', 'G', 'B')
```

There was little doubt in our minds that the three pixel values were red level, green level, and blue level. We've used the `getband()` method to get confirmation from Pillow that our assumption about the image encoding band was correct.

We now have access to the individual bytes of the image. The next steps are to get the bits from our secret message and then adulterate the image bytes with our secret message bits.

Extracting bytes from Unicode characters

In order to encode our secret message into the bytes of an image, we'll need to transform our Unicode message into bytes. Once we have some bytes, we can then make one more transformation to get a sequence of bits.

The second question, is how do we get the individual bits of the message text? Another form of this question is, how do we turn a string of Unicode characters into a string of individual bits?

Here's a Unicode string we can work with: `http://www.kearsarge.navy.mil`. We'll break the transformation into two steps: first to bytes and then to bits. There are a number of ways to encode strings as bytes. We'll use the UTF-8 encoding as that's very popular:

```
>>> message="http://www.kearsarge.navy.mil"
>>> message.encode("UTF-8")
b'http://www.kearsarge.navy.mil'
```

It doesn't look like too much happened there. This is because the UTF-8 encoding happens to match the ASCII encoding that Python byte literals use. This means that the bytes version of a string, which happens to use only US-ASCII characters, will look very much like the original Python string. The presence of special `b'  '` quotes is the hint that the string is only bytes, not full Unicode characters.

If we had some non-ASCII Unicode characters in our string, then the UTF-8 encoding would become quite a bit more complex.

Just for reference, here's the UTF-16 encoding of our message:

```
>>> message.encode("UTF-16")
b'\xff\xfeh\x00t\x00t\x00p\x00:\x00/\x00/\x00w\x00w\x00w\x00.\x00k\
x00e\x00a\x00r
\x00s\x00a\x00r\x00g\x00e\x00.\x00n\x00a\x00v\x00y\x00.\x00m\x00i\
x00l\x00'
```

The previous encoded message looks to be a proper mess. As expected, it's close to twice as big as UTF-8.

Here's another view of the individual bytes in the message:

```
>>> [ hex(c) for c in message.encode("UTF-8") ]
['0x68', '0x74', '0x74', '0x70', '0x3a', '0x2f', '0x2f', '0x77',
 '0x77', '0x77', '0x2e', '0x6b', '0x65', '0x61', '0x72', '0x73',
 '0x61', '0x72', '0x67', '0x65', '0x2e', '0x6e', '0x61', '0x76',
 '0x79', '0x2e', '0x6d', '0x69', '0x6c']
```

We've used a generator expression to apply the `hex()` function to each byte. This gives us a hint as to how we're going to proceed. Our message was transformed into 29 bytes, which is 232 bits; we want to put these bits into the first 232 pixels of our image.

Manipulating bits and bytes

As we'll be fiddling with individual bits, we need to know how to transform a Python byte into a tuple of 8 bits. The inverse is a technique to transform an 8-bit tuple back into a single byte. If we expand each byte into an eight-tuple, we can easily adjust the bits and confirm that we're doing the right thing.

We'll need some functions to expand a list of byte into bits and contract the bits back to the original list of bytes. Then, we can apply these functions to our sequence of bytes to create the sequence of individual bits.

The essential computer science is explained next:

A number, n, is a polynomial in some particular base. Here's the polynomial for the value of 234 with base 10:

$$234 = 2 \times 10^2 + 3 \times 10^1 + 4 \times 10^0 = 200 + 30 + 4$$

In base 16, we have $234 = 14 \times 16^1 + 10 \times 16^0$. When writing hex, we use letters for the 14 and 10 digits: `0xea`.

This kind of polynomial representation is true in base 2. A number, n, is a polynomial in base 2. Here's the polynomial for the value of 234:

$$234 = 1 \times 2^7 + 1 \times 2^6 + 1 \times 2^5 + 0 \times 2^4 + 1 \times 2^3 + 0 \times 2^2 + 1 \times 2^1 + 0 \times 2^0$$

Here's a way to extract the lower 8 bits from a numeric value:

```
def to_bits( v ):
    b= []
    for i in range(8):
        b.append( v & 1 )
        v >>= 1
    return tuple(reversed(b))
```

The `v&1` expression applies a bitwise operation to extract the rightmost bit of a number. We'll append the calculated bit value to the b variable. The `v >>= 1` statement is the same as `v = v>>1`; the `v>>1` expression will shift the value, v, one bit to the right. After doing this eight times, we've extracted the lowest bits of the v value. We've assembled this sequence of bits in a list object, b.

The results are accumulated in the *wrong* order, so we reverse them and create a tidy little eight-tuple object. We can compare this with the built-in `bin()` function:

```
>>> to_bits(234)
(1, 1, 1, 0, 1, 0, 1, 0)
>>> bin(234)
'0b11101010'
```

For a value over 127, both the `bin()` and `to_bits()` functions produce 8-bit results. For smaller values, we'll see that the `bin()` function doesn't produce 8 bits; it produces just enough bits.

The opposite transformation evaluates the polynomial. We can do a little algebra to optimize the number of multiplications:

$$234 = ((((((1 \times 2) + 1) \times 2 + 1) \times 2 + 0) \times 2 + 1) \times 2 + 0) \times 2 + 1) \times 2 + 0$$

Because of the grouping, the leftmost 1 winds up multiplied by 2^7. As shifting bits to the left is the same as multiplying by 2, we can reconstruct the a byte value from a tuple of bits as follows:

```
def to_byte( b ):
    v= 0
    for bit in b:
        v = (v<<1)|bit
    return v
```

The `(v<<1)|bit` expression will shift v to the left 1 bit, effectively performing a `*2` operation. An OR operation will fold the next bit into the value being accumulated.

We can test these two functions with a loop like this:

```
for test in range(256):
    b = to_bits(test)
    v = to_byte(b)
    assert v == test
```

If all 256 byte values are converted to bits and back to bytes, we are absolutely sure that we can convert bytes to bits. We can use this to see the expansion of our message:

```
message_bytes = message.encode("UTF-8")
print( list(to_bits(c) for c in message_bytes) )
```

This will show us a big list of 8-tuples:

```
[(1, 1, 1, 1, 1, 1, 1, 1), (1, 1, 1, 1, 1, 1, 1, 0),
 (0, 1, 1, 0, 1, 0, 0, 0), (0, 0, 0, 0, 0, 0, 0, 0),
   ...
 (0, 1, 1, 0, 1, 1, 0, 0), (0, 0, 0, 0, 0, 0, 0, 0)]
```

Each byte of the secret message has become an eight-tuple of individual bits.

Assembling the bits

At this point, we've got two parallel sequences of values:

- The bytes from the image (ideally enough to encode our entire message)
- The bits from our secret message (in the example, we've got just 29 bytes, which is 232 bits)

The idea is to step through each byte of the image and incorporate one bit of the secret message into that byte.

Before we can fully tweak the various image bytes with our message bits, we need to assemble a long sequence of individual bits. We have two choices to do this. We can create a `list` object with all of the bit values. This wastes a bit of memory, and we can do better.

We can also create a generator function that will appear to be a `sequence` object with all of the bits.

Here's a generator function that we can use to emit the entire sequence of bits from the message:

```
def bit_sequence( list_of_tuples ):
    for t8 in list_of_tuples:
        for b in t8:
            yield b
```

We've stepped through each individual eight-tuple in the list-of-tuples values that can be created by our `to_bits()` function. For each bit in the 8-tuple, we've used the `yield` statement to provide the individual bit values. Any expression or statement that expects an iterable sequence will be able to use this function.

Here's how we can use this to accumulate a sequence of all 232 bits from a message:

```
print( list( bit_sequence(
    (to_bits(c) for c in message_bytes)
) ) )
```

This will apply the `to_bits()` function to each byte of the message, creating a sequence of 8-tuples. Then it will apply the `bit_sequence()` generator to that sequence of eight-tuples. The output is a sequence of individual bits, which we collected into a `list` object. The resulting list looks like this:

```
[1, 1, 1, 1, 1, 1, 1, 1, 1, 1, 1, 1, 1, 1, 1, 0,
0, 1, 1, 0, 1, 0, 0, 0, 0, 0, 0, 0, 0, 0, 0, 0,
...
0, 1, 1, 0, 1, 1, 0, 0, 0, 0, 0, 0, 0, 0, 0, 0]
```

We can see the list of 232 individual bits built from our original message.

Here's the inverse to the `bit_sequence()` function. This will group a sequence of bits into eight-tuples:

```
def byte_sequence( bits ):
    byte= []
    for n, b in enumerate(bits):
        if n%8 == 0 and n != 0:
            yield to_byte(byte)
            byte= []
        byte.append( b )
    yield to_byte(byte)
```

We've used the built-in `enumerate()` generator function to provide a number for each individual bit in the original sequence. The output from the `enumerate(bits)` expression is a sequence of two-tuples; each two-tuple has the enumerated bit number (from 0 to 231) and the bit value itself (0 or 1).

When the bit number is a multiple of 8 (`n%8 == 0`), we've seen a complete batch of eight bits. We can convert these eight bits to a byte with `to_byte()`, yield the byte value, and reset our temporary accumulator, `byte`, to be empty.

 We've made a special exception for the very first byte.

The `enumerate()` function will assign the very first byte number 0; since `0%8 == 0`, it looks like we've just accumulated eight bits to make a byte. We've avoided this complication by assuring that n is not 0; it's not the first bit value. We could also have used the `len(byte) != 0` expression to avoid the first-time complication.

The final `yield` statement is critical for success. The final batch of bits will have `n%8` values of 0 to 7. The `n%8` test won't be used when the collection of bits is exhausted, but we'll still have eight bits accumulated in the `byte` variable. We yield this final batch of eight bits as an extra step.

Here's what it looks like:

```
>>> list(byte_sequence(bits))
[255, 254, 104, 0, 116, 0, 116, 0, 112, 0, 58, 0, 47, 0, 47, 0, 119,
0, 119, 0, 119, 0, 46, 0, 107, 0, 101, 0, 97, 0, 114, 0, 115, 0, 97,
0, 114, 0, 103, 0, 101, 0, 46, 0, 110, 0, 97, 0, 118, 0, 121, 0, 46,
0, 109, 0, 105, 0, 108, 0]
```

We've taken the sequence of individual bits and collected each batch of eight bits into bytes.

Encoding the message

Now that we can transform any Unicode string into bits, we can encode a message into an image. The final nuance is how to delimit the message. We don't want to accidentally decode each byte in the entire image. If we did this, our message will be padded with random characters. We need to know when to stop decoding.

One common technique is to include a terminator character. Another common technique is to provide a length in front of the string. We're going to include a length in front of the string so that we aren't constrained by the contents of the string or the encoded bytes that are produced from that string.

We'll use a 2-byte length in front of the string; we can encode it into bytes and bits like this:

```
len_H, len_L = divmod( len(message), 256 )
size = [to_bits(len_H), to_bits(len_L)]
```

We've used the Python `divmod()` function to compute the quotient and remainder after division. The results of the `divmod( len(message), 256 )` expression will be `len(message)//256` and `len(message)%256`. We can recover the original value from the `len_H*256+len_L` expression.

The `size` variable is set to a short sequence composed of two eight-tuples built from the `len_H` and `len_L` values.

The complete sequence of bytes, including the length, looks like this:

```
message_bytes= message.encode("UTF-8")
bits_list = list(to_bits(c) for c in message_bytes )
len_h, len_l = divmod( len(message_bytes), 256 )
size_list = [to_bits(len_h), to_bits(len_l)]
bit_sequence( size_list+bits_list )
```

First, we encoded the message into bytes. Depending on the Unicode characters involved and the encoding used, this may be longer than the original message. The `bits_list` variable is a sequence of eight-tuples built from the various bytes of the encoded message.

Then, we created two more bytes with the length information and converted them to bits. The `size_list` variable is a sequence of eight-tuples built from the bytes of the encoded size.

The `size_list+bits_list` expression shows how to concatenate the two sequences to create a long sequence of individual bits that we can embed into our image.

Here's how we use the `putpixel()` and `getpixel()` methods to update the image:

```
w, h = ship.size
for p,m in enumerate( bit_sequence(size_list+bits_list) ):
    y, x = divmod( p, w )
    r, g, b = ship.getpixel( (x,y) )
    r_new = (r & 0xfe) | m
    print( (r, g, b), m, (r_new, g, b) )
    ship.putpixel( (x,y), (r_new, g, b)  )
```

We've extracted the size of the original image; this tells us how long the *x* axis is so that we can use multiple rows of the image if necessary. If our image only has 128 pixels on a row, we'll need more than one row for a 292-bit message.

We've applied the `enumerate()` function to the `bit_sequence(size_list+bits_list)` value. This will provide both a sequence number and an individual bit from the original message. The sequence number can be converted to a row and column using the `divmod()` function. We'll set `y` to `sequence // width`; we'll set `x` to `sequence % width`.

If we use the thumbnail image, which is 128-pixels wide, the first 128 bits go to row `0`. The next 128 bits go to row `1`. The balance of the 292 bits will wind up on row `3`.

We got the RGB values from the pixel using `ship.getpixel( (x,y) )`.

We've highlighted the bit-fiddling part: `r_new = (r & 0xfe) | m`. This uses a **mask** value of `0xfe`, which is `0b11111110`. This works because the `&` operator has a handy feature. When we use `b&1`, the value of `b` is preserved. When we use `b&0`, the result is `0`.

Try it, as shown in the following code:

```
>>> 1 & 1
1
>>> 0 & 1
0
```

The value of `b` (either `1` or `0`) was preserved. Similarly, `1 & 0` and `0 & 0` are both `0`.

Using a mask value in `(r & 0xfe)` means that the leftmost seven bits of `r` will be preserved; the rightmost bit will be set to `0`. When we use `(r & 0xfe) | m`, we'll be folding the value of `m` into the rightmost position. We've printed out the old and new pixel values to provide some details on how this works. Here are two rows from the output:

```
(245, 247, 246) 0 (244, 247, 246)
(246, 248, 247) 1 (247, 248, 247)
```

We can see that the old value of the red channel was 245:

```
>>> 245 & 0xfe
244
>>> (245 & 0xfe) | 0
244
```

The value 244 shows how the rightmost bit was removed from 245. When we fold in a new bit value 0, the result remains 244. An even value encodes a 0 bit from our secret message.

In this case, the old value of the red channel was 246:

```
>>> 246 & 0xfe
246
>>> (246 & 0xfe) | 1
247
```

The value remains 246 when we remove the rightmost bit. When we fold in a new bit value of 1, the result becomes 247. An odd value encodes a one bit from our secret message.

 Using `ship.show()` before and after the image reveals no perceivable change to the image.

After all, we've only tweaked the level of the red in the image by plus or minus 1 on a scale of 256, less than half percent change.

Decoding a message

We will decode a message concealed with steganography in two steps. The first step will decode just the first two bytes of length information, so we can recover our embedded message. Once we know how many bytes we're looking for, we can decode the right number of bits, recovering just our embedded characters, and nothing more.

As we'll be dipping into the message twice, it will help to write a bit extractor. Here's the function that will strip bits from the red channel of an image:

```
def get_bits( image, offset= 0, size= 16 ):
    w, h = image.size
    for p in range(offset, offset+size):
        y, x = divmod( p, w )
        r, g, b = image.getpixel( (x,y) )
        yield r & 0x01
```

We've defined a function with three parameters: an image, an offset into the image, and a number of bits to extract. The length information is an offset zero and has a length of 16 bits. We set those as default values.

We used the a common `divmod()` calculation to transform a position into y and x coordinates based on the overall width of the image. The y value is `position// width`; the x value is `position%width`. This matches the calculation carried out when embedding bits into the message.

We used the image's `getpixel()` method to extract the three channels of color information. We used `r & 0x01` to calculate just the rightmost bit of the red channel.

As the value was returned with a `yield` statement, this is a generator function: it provides a sequence of values. As our `byte_sequence()` function expects a sequence of values, we can combine the two to extract the size, as shown in the following code:

```
size_H, size_L = byte_sequence( get_bits( ship, 0, 16 ) )
size= size_H*256+size_L
```

We grabbed 16 bits from the image using the `get_bits()` function. This sequence of bits was provided to the `byte_sequence()` function. The bits were grouped into eight-tuples and the eight-tuples transformed into single values. We can then multiply and add these values to recover the original message size.

Now that we know how many bytes to get, we also know how many bits to extract. The extraction looks like this:

```
message= byte_sequence(get_bits(ship, 16, size*8))
```

We've used the `get_bits()` function to extract bits starting from position 16 and extending until we've found a total of `size*8` individual bits. We grouped the bits into eight-tuples and converted the eight-tuples to individual values.

Given a sequence of bytes, we can create a `bytes` object and use Python's decoder to recover the original string. It looks like this:

```
print( bytes(message).decode("UTF-8") )
```

This will properly decode bytes into characters using the UTF-8 encoding.

Detecting and preventing tampering

We can use steganography to assure that our message isn't tampered with. If we can't find our digital watermark properly encoded, we know that our picture was touched. This is one way to detect tampering. A more robust technique to detect tampering is to use hash totals. There are a number of hash algorithms used to produce a summary or signature of a sequence of bytes. We send both the message and the hash code separately. If the received message doesn't match the hash code, we know something went wrong. One common use case for hashes is to confirm a proper download of a file. After downloading a file, we should compare the hash of the file we got with a separately published hash value; if the hash values don't match, something's wrong with the file. We can delete it before opening it.

While it seems like encryption would prevent tampering, it requires careful management of the encryption keys. Encryption is no panacea. It's possible to employ a good encryption algorithm but lose control of the keys, rendering the encryption useless. Someone with unauthorized access to the key can rewrite the file and no one would know.

Using hash totals to validate a file

Python has a number of hash algorithms available in the hashlib module. Software downloads are often provided with MD5 hashes of the software package. We can compute an MD5 digest of a file using hashlib, as shown in the following code:

```
import hashlib
md5 = hashlib.new("md5")
with open( "LHD_warship.jpg", "rb" ) as some_file:
    md5.update( some_file.read() )
print( md5.hexdigest() )
```

We've created an MD5 digest object using the hashlib.new() function; we named the algorithm to be used. We opened the file in *bytes* mode. We provided the entire file to the digest object's update() method. For really large files, we might want to read the file in blocks rather than read the entire file into memory in one swoop. Finally, we printed the hex version of the digest.

This will provide a hexadecimal string version of the MD5 digest, as follows:

```
0032e5b0d9dd6e3a878a611b49807d24
```

Having this secure hash allows us to confirm that the file has not been tampered with in its journey through the Internet from sender to receiver.

Using a key with a digest

We can provide considerably more security by adding a key to a message digest. This doesn't encrypt the message; it encrypts the digest to be sure that the digest is not touched during transmission.

The `hmac` module in the Python standard library handles this for us, as shown in the following code:

```
import hmac
with open( "LHD_warship.jpg", "rb" ) as some_file:
    keyed= hmac.new( b"Agent Garbo", some_file.read() )
print( keyed.hexdigest() )
```

In this example, we've created an HMAC digest object and also passed the message content to that digest object. The `hmac.new()` function can accept both the key (as a string of bytes) and the body of a message.

The hex digest from this HMAC digest object includes both the original message and a key we provided. Here's the output:

```
42212d077cc5232f3f2da007d35a726c
```

As HQ knows our key, they can confirm that a message comes from us.

Similarly, HQ must use our key when sending us a message. We can then use our key when we read the message to confirm that it was sent to us by HQ.

Solving problems – encrypting a message

For proper encryption, the PyCrypto package can be used, which can be downloaded from `https://www.dlitz.net/software/pycrypto/`. As with Pillow, this is a hefty download.

As we saw in *Chapter 1, Our Espionage Toolkit*, a poor choice of key will render any encryption scheme essentially worthless. If we encrypt a file using a single-word key that's available in a readily available corpus of words, we haven't really made our data very secure at all. A brute-force attack will break the encryption.

We can combine steganography with the creation of a `ZipFile` archive to embed a message in an image in a ZIP file. As a ZIP file can have a comment string, we can include an HMAC signature as the comment for the ZIP archive.

Ideally, we'd use the ZIP encryption. However, the Python `ZipFile` library doesn't create encrypted ZIP files. It only reads encrypted files.

We're going to define a function that looks like this:

```
def package( text, image_source, key_hmac, filename ):
```

We'll provide the text of our message, the image source, the key we'll use to create our HMAC signature, and an output filename. The output from this will be a ZIP file that contains the image and the signature.

The outline of our `package()` function looks like this:

```
image= Image.open( image_source )
steg_embed( image, text )
image.save( "/tmp/package.tiff", format="TIFF" )
with open("/tmp/package.tiff","rb") as saved:
    digest= hmac.new( key_hmac.encode("ASCII"), saved.read() )
with ZipFile( filename, "w" ) as archive:
    archive.write( "/tmp/package.tiff", "image.tiff" )
    archive.comment= digest.hexdigest().encode("ASCII")
os.remove( "/tmp/package.tiff" )
```

We've opened the source image and used an `steg_embed()` function to put our secret message into the image. We've saved the updated image to a temporary file.

We computed the HMAC digest of our image file before doing anything else with it. We saved the digest in the `digest` variable.

Now that everything is prepared, we can create a new archive file. We can write the image into one member of the archive. When we are setting the `comment` attribute of the archive, this will make sure that the comment text is written when the archive is closed.

Note that we had to convert the key to ASCII bytes to create a digest. The HMAC algorithm is defined for bytes, not Unicode characters. Similarly, the resulting `hexdigest()` string had to be converted to ASCII bytes before it could be placed in the archive. ZIP archives only work in bytes and can't directly support Unicode characters.

Finally, we removed the temporary file that had the tweaked image in it. There's no reason to leave potentially incriminating files laying around.

For this to work, we need to complete the function, `steg_embed()`, that implements our steganographic encoding. See the *Some approaches to steganography* section for details on how this needs to work.

Unpacking a message

We'll also need the inverse function that can decode a message in a ZIP archive. This function would have a definition like this:

```
def unpackage( filename, key_hmac ):
```

It requires a ZIP filename and a key to validate the signature. This can return two things: the embedded message and the image into which the message was encoded.

The outline of our `unpackage()` function looks like this:

```
    try:
        os.remove( "/tmp/image.tiff" )
    except FileNotFoundError:
        pass
    with ZipFile( filename, "r" ) as archive:
        with archive.open( "image.tiff", "r" ) as member:
            keyed= hmac.new( key_hmac.encode("ASCII"), member.read() )
            assert archive.comment == keyed.hexdigest().encode("ASCII"),
"Invalid HMAC"
            archive.extract( "image.tiff", "/tmp" )
        image= Image.open( "/tmp/image.tiff" )
        text= steg_extract( image )
        os.remove( "/tmp/image.tiff" )
        return text, image
```

We're going to remove any temporary file that might exist. If the file doesn't exist already, that's a good thing, but it will raise a `FileNotFoundError` exception. We need to trap and silence that exception.

Our first step is to open the ZIP file and then open the `image.tiff` member within the ZIP file. We compute the HMAC digest of this member. Then, we assert that the archive comment matches the hex digest of the selected member. If the condition in the `assert` statement is false and the HMAC keys don't match, then this will raise an exception and the script will stop running. This will also mean that our message was compromised. If the condition in the `assert` statement is true, it executes silently.

If the assertion is true, we can extract the image file to a spot in the `/tmp` directory. From here, we can open the file and use the `steg_extract()` function to recover the message hidden in the image. Windows agents can use the `os` module to locate a temporary directory. The value of `os.environ['TEMP']` will name a suitable temporary directory.

Once we've got the message, we can remove the temporary file.

For this to work, we need to complete the function, `steg_extract()`, that implements our steganographic decoding. See the *Some approaches to steganography* section for details on how this needs to work.

Summary

In this chapter, we learned how to work on a computer's filesystem and common file formats. We looked in depth at image files. We also saw how Pillow allows us to apply operations such as cropping, filtering, and enhancing to an image.

We covered Python bit-fiddling operators such as &, |, <<, and >>. These operators work on the individual bits of an integer value. Something like `bin(0b0100 & 0b1100)` will show how the answer is based on doing an AND operation on each individual bit of the number.

We also looked at how we can apply steganographic techniques to conceal a message in an image file. This involved both byte and bit manipulation in Python.

In the next chapter, we'll look at incorporating geolocation information with our other information gathering. We know that pictures can be tied to locations, so geocoding and reverse geocoding are essential. We'll also look at ways to read more complex online datasets and combine multiple web services into a composite application.

4
Drops, Hideouts, Meetups, and Lairs

We'll extend some of the techniques introduced in *Chapter 2*, *Acquiring Intelligence Data*, to make RESTful web service requests for geocoding. This will allow us to pinpoint various kinds of secret locations. This will also build on image location processing from *Chapter 3*, *Encoding Secret Messages with Steganography*.

We will look at some online datasets that will lead us to more techniques in data gathering. In order to work with a wide variety of data, we will need to add an HTML parser to our toolkit. We'll download BeautifulSoup, since it's very good at tracking down the information buried in HTML pages.

In this chapter, we'll also look at some more sophisticated Python algorithms. We'll start with geocoding services to translate address and latitude-longitude coordinates.

We'll look at the **haversine** formula to compute distances between locations. This will mean using the `math` library to access trigonometric functions.

We'll learn about the various kinds of grid coding schemes, which will help us reduce the complexity of latitude and longitude. These coding schemes will show us a number of data representation techniques. This chapter will show ways to compress numbers via a change in representation.

We'll see ways to parse HTML `<table>` tags and create Python collections that we can work with. We'll also look at online data sources that provide clean data in the JSON format. This can be easier to gather and work with.

Our goal is to use Python to combine multiple online services. This will allow us to integrate geocoding and data analysis. With that information, we can locate the best place to meet our contacts without traveling too far from our secret base of operations.

Background briefing – latitude, longitude, and GPS

Before we can get geographic information, we'll need to review some essential terminology. One powerful piece of modern technology that helps civilians as well as secret agents is the **Global Positioning System (GPS)**, a satellite-based system to determine location. The GPS allows a terrestrial device to pinpoint its location in both space and time.

The idea underlying GPS is quite elegant. Each satellite produces a stream of data that includes position and super accurate timestamps. A receiver with multiple streams of data can plug the positions and timestamps into a matrix of simultaneous equations to determine the receiver's position with respect to the various satellites. Given enough satellites, a receiver can precisely calculate latitude, longitude, elevation, and even the current time.

For more information see `http://en.wikipedia.org/wiki/Global_Positioning_System#Navigation_equations`.

A position's latitude is an angle measured relative to the equator and poles. We must provide the direction for this angle: N or S for latitude. For example, 36°50'40.12"N is given in degrees (°), minutes ('), and seconds (") with the all-important N to show which side of the equator the position is on.

We can also state latitude as 36°50.6687'N using degrees and minutes; or, we could use 36.844478, known as using decimal degrees. Directions toward the north are written in positive angles. Directions to the south are negative. The underlying `math` library works in radians, but radians are not widely used to display positions to humans.

Longitude is an angle east of the **prime meridian** or the **Greenwich meridian**. Angles to the west of Greenwich are stated as negative numbers. Consequently, 76°17'35.21"W can also be stated as -76.293114.

When we look at a globe, we notice that the latitude lines are all parallel with the equator. Each degree of latitude is about 60 nautical miles in the north-south direction.

The longitude lines, however, all intersect at the north and south pole. Those north-south lines are not parallel. On a map or a nautical chart, however, a distortion (actually known as a **projection**) is used so that the longitude lines are parallel to each other. With our usual experience of driving short distances on land, the distortion doesn't matter much, since we're often constrained to driving on highways that wander around rivers and mountains. What's important is that the rectangular grid of a map is handy, but misleading. Simple analytical plane geometry isn't appropriate. Hence, we have to switch to spherical geometry.

Coping with GPS device limitations

A GPS receiver needs to receive data from a number of satellites concurrently; a minimum of three satellites can be used for triangulation. There may be interference with microwave signals indoors, and even outdoors in urban environments, making it difficult (or impossible) to get enough data to properly compute the receiver's location. Tall buildings and other obstructions such as walls, prevent the direct signal access needed for accuracy. It may take a long time to acquire enough high-quality satellite signals to compute a position.

A common workaround to the satellite visibility problem is to rely on cellular telephone towers as a way to compute a position very quickly even without GPS satellite data. A phone which is in contact with several cell towers can have the position triangulated based on the overlapping transmission patterns. In many telephone devices, the GPS calculation requires local cellphone towers before it can calculate a GPS position.

There are many non-phone GPS devices that can be directly connected to a computer to get accurate GPS fixes without relying on cellular data. Navigation computers (mariners call them **chart plotters**) work without the need to connect to a cellular network. In many cases, we can use modules such as `pyserial` to extract data from these devices.

See `http://pyserial.sourceforge.net` for more information on the pySerial project and how we can use this read data from a GPS device via a serial to a USB adapter.

Handling politics – borders, precincts, jurisdictions, and neighborhoods

Borders create endless problems—some profound, some subtle. The entire sweep of human history seems to center on borders and wars. The edges of neighborhoods are often subjective. In an urban environment, a block or two may not matter much when discussing the difference between Los Feliz and East Hollywood. On the other hand, this kind of knowledge is what defines the *local* restaurants as recognized by people who live there.

When it comes to more formal definitions—such as election districts at city, state, and federal levels—the side of the street may have profound implications. In some cities, this political division information is readily available via RESTful web service requests. In other locales, this information is buried in a drawer somewhere, or published in some kind of hard-to-process PDF document.

Some media companies provide neighborhood information. The LA Times Data Desk, for example, has a fairly rigorous definition of the various neighborhoods around the greater Los Angeles area. For excellent background information on how to work with this kind of information, see `http://www.latimes.com/local/datadesk/`.

Finding out where we are with geocoding services

We'll use some geocoding services to get answers to the following questions:

- What's the latitude and longitude of a given street address? This is called address geocoding or simply geocoding.

- Which street address is closest to a given latitude and longitude? This is called reverse geocoding.

There are, of course, many more questions we could ask. We might want to know a route to navigate between two addresses. We might want to know what public transportation choices we have to get from one place to another. For now, we'll limit ourselves to these two essential geocoding questions.

There are many geocoding services available on the World wide web (WWW). There are a number of terms related to geocoding, including geomarketing, geo targeting, geolocation, and geotagging. They're all essentially similar; they depict location-based information. It can take a fair amount of espionage to track down a service with the features we want.

The following link gives a list of services:

`http://geoservices.tamu.edu/Services/Geocode/OtherGeocoders/`

This list is far from definitive. Some of the services listed here don't work very well. Some large companies aren't listed; for example, MapQuest appears to be missing. See `http://mapquest.com` for more information.

Most geocoding services want to track usage. For large batches of requests, they want to be paid for the services they offer. Consequently, they issue credentials (a key) that must be part of every request. The procedure to get a key varies from service to service.

We'll look closely at the services offered by Google. They offer a limited service without the overhead of requesting credentials. Instead of asking us to get a key, they'll throttle our requests if we make too much use of their service.

Geocoding an address

The forward geocoding service from address to latitude and longitude can be accessed via Python's urllib.request module. For a quick review, see the *Using a REST API in Python* section of *Chapter 2, Acquiring Intelligence Data*. This is usually a three-step process.

Define the parts of the URL. It helps to separate the static portions from the dynamic query portion. We need to use the urllib.parse.urlencode() function to encode the query string.

Open the URL using a with statement context. This will send the request and get the response. The JSON document must be parsed in this with context.

Process the object that was received. This is done outside the with context. Here's what it looks like:

```python
import urllib.request
import urllib.parse
import json

# 1. Build the URL.
form = {
    "address": "333 waterside drive, norfolk, va, 23510",
    "sensor": "false",
    #"key": Provide the API Key here if you're registered,
}
query = urllib.parse.urlencode(form, safe=",")
scheme_netloc_path = "https://maps.googleapis.com/maps/api/geocode/json"
print(scheme_netloc_path+"?"+query)

# 2. Send the request; get the response.
with urllib.request.urlopen(scheme_netloc_path+"?"+query) as geocode:
    print(geocode.info())
    response= json.loads( geocode.read().decode("UTF-8") )

# 3. Process the response object.
print(response)
```

We have created a dictionary with the two required fields: address and sensor. If you want to sign up with Google for additional support and higher-volume requests, you can get an API key. It will become a third field in the request dictionary. We used a # comment to include a reminder about the use of the key item.

An HTML web page form is essentially this kind of dictionary with names and values. When the browser makes a request, the form is encoded before it is transmitted to the web server. Our Python program does this using `urllib.parse.urlencode()` to encode the form data into something that a web server can use.

 Google requires us to use the `safe=","` parameter. This assures us that the `","` characters in the address will be preserved instead of being rewritten as `"%2C"`.

A complete URL has a scheme, location, path, and an optional query. The scheme, location, and path tend to remain fixed. We assembled a complete URL from the fixed portions and the dynamic query content, printed it, and also used it as an argument to the `urllib.request.urlopen()` function.

In the `with` statement, we created a processing context. This will send the request and read the response. Inside the `with` context, we printed the headers to confirm that the request worked. More importantly, we loaded the JSON response, which will create a Python object. We saved that object in the `response` variable.

After creating the Python object, we can release the resources tied up in making the geocoding request. Leaving the indented block of the `with` statement assures that all the resources are released and the file-like response is closed.

After the `with` context, we can work with the response. In this case, we merely print the object. Later, we'll do more with the response.

We'll see three things, as shown in the following snippet—the URL that we built, headers from the HTTP response, and finally the geocoding output as a JSON-formatted document:

```
https://maps.googleapis.com/maps/api/geocode/json?sensor=false&address
=333+waterside+drive,+norfolk,+va,+23510

Content-Type: application/json; charset=UTF-8
Date: Sun, 13 Jul 2014 11:49:48 GMT
Expires: Mon, 14 Jul 2014 11:49:48 GMT
Cache-Control: public, max-age=86400
Vary: Accept-Language
Access-Control-Allow-Origin: *
Server: mafe
X-XSS-Protection: 1; mode=block
X-Frame-Options: SAMEORIGIN
Alternate-Protocol: 443:quic
Connection: close
```

```
{'results': [{'address_components': [{'long_name': '333',
                                      'short_name': '333',
                                      'types': ['street_number']},
                                     {'long_name': 'Waterside Festival
Marketplace',
                                      'short_name': 'Waterside
Festival Marketplace',
                                      'types': ['establishment']},
                                     {'long_name': 'Waterside Drive',
                                      'short_name': 'Waterside Dr',
                                      'types': ['route']},
                                     {'long_name': 'Norfolk',
                                      'short_name': 'Norfolk',
                                      'types': ['locality',
'political']},
                                     {'long_name': 'Virginia',
                                      'short_name': 'VA',
                                      'types': ['administrative_area_
level_1',
                                                'political']},
                                     {'long_name': 'United States',
                                      'short_name': 'US',
                                      'types': ['country',
'political']},
                                     {'long_name': '23510',
                                      'short_name': '23510',
                                      'types': ['postal_code']}],
              'formatted_address': '333 Waterside Drive, Waterside
Festival Marketplace, Norfolk, VA 23510, USA',
              'geometry': {'location': {'lat': 36.844305,
                                        'lng': -76.29111999999999},
                           'location_type': 'ROOFTOP',
                           'viewport': {'northeast': {'lat':
36.84565398029149,
                                                      'lng':
-76.28977101970848},
                                        'southwest': {'lat':
36.8429560197085,
                                                      'lng':
-76.29246898029149}}},
              'types': ['street_address']}],
 'status': 'OK'}
{'lng': -76.29111999999999, 'lat': 36.844305}
```

The JSON document can be loaded using the `json` module. This will create a dictionary with two keys: `results` and `status`. In our example, we loaded the dictionary into a variable named `response`. The value of `response['results']` is a list of dictionaries. Since we only requested one address, we only expect one element in this list. Most of what we want, then, is in `response['results'][0]`.

When we examine that structure, we find a subdictionary with four keys. Of those, the `'geometry'` key has the geocoding latitude and longitude information.

We can extend this script to access the location details using the following code:

```
print( response['results'][0]['geometry']['location'])
```

This provides us with a small dictionary that looks like this:

```
{'lat': 36.844305, 'lng': -76.29111999999999}
```

This is what we wanted to know about the street address.

Also, as a purely technical note on the Python language, we included # comments to show the important steps in our algorithm. A comment starts with # and goes to the end of the line. In this example, the comments are on the lines by themselves. In general, they can be placed at the end of any line of code.

Specifically, we called this out with a comment:

```
form = {
    "address": "333 waterside drive, norfolk, va, 23510",
    "sensor": "false",
    #"key": Provide the API Key here if you're registered,
}
```

The form dictionary has two keys. A third key can be added by removing the # comment indicator and filling in the API key that Google has supplied.

Reverse geocoding a latitude-longitude point

The reverse geocoding service locates nearby addresses from a latitude and longitude position. This kind of query involves a certain amount of inherent ambiguity. A point that's midway between two large buildings, for example, could be associated with either or both buildings. Also, we might be interested in different levels of details: rather than a street address, we may only wish to know the state or country for a particular position.

Here's what this web service request looks like:

```
import urllib.request
import urllib.parse
import json

# 1. Build the URL.
form = {
    "latlng": "36.844305,-76.29112",
    "sensor": "false",
    #"key": Provide the API Key here if you're registered ,
}
query = urllib.parse.urlencode(form, safe=",")
scheme_netloc_path = "https://maps.googleapis.com/maps/api/geocode/
json"
print(scheme_netloc_path+"?"+query)

# 2.  Send the request; get the response
with urllib.request.urlopen(scheme_netloc_path+"?"+query) as geocode:
    print(geocode.info())
    response= json.loads( geocode.read().decode("UTF-8") )

# 3. Process the response object.
for alt in response['results']:
    print(alt['types'], alt['formatted_address'])
```

The form has two required fields: latlng and sensor.

Signing up with Google for additional support and higher-volume requests requires an API key. It would become a third field in the request form; we have left a # comment in the code as a reminder.

We encoded the form data and assigned it to the query variable. The safe="," parameter assures us that the "," characters in the latitude-longitude pair will be preserved instead of being rewritten into a %2C escape code.

We assembled a complete address from the fixed portions of the URL (the scheme, net location, and path) plus the dynamic query content. The scheme, location, and path are generally fixed. The query is encoded from the form data.

In the with statement, we created a processing context to send the request and read the response. Inside the with context, we displayed the headers and loaded the resulting JSON document, creating a Python object. Once we have the Python object, we can exit the processing context and release the resources.

The response is a Python dictionary. There are two keys: `'results'` and `'status'`. The value of `response['results']` is a list of dictionaries. There are a number of alternative addresses in the `results` list. Each result is a dictionary with two interesting keys: the `'types'` key, which shows the type of address and the `'formatted_address'` key, which is a well-formatted address close to the given location.

The output looks like this:

```
['street_address'] 333 Waterside Drive, Waterside Festival
Marketplace, Norfolk, VA 23510, USA
['postal_code'] Norfolk, VA 23510, USA
['locality', 'political'] Norfolk, VA, USA
['administrative_area_level_1', 'political'] Virginia, USA
['country', 'political'] United States
```

Each of the alternatives shows a hierarchy of nested political containers for the address: postal code, locality, state (called `administrative_area_level_1`), and country.

How close? What direction?

In order to calculate the distance between two points, we'll need to use some spherical geometry calculations. The problem we will have to overcome is that our charts and maps are flat. But the actual planet is very close to being spherical. While the spherical geometry may be a bit advanced, the programming is pretty simple. It will show us several features of the Python `math` library.

The distance between two latitude and longitude points on a sphere is defined as follows:

$$d = \arccos\left[\sin(lat_1) \times \sin(lat_2) + \cos(lat_1) \times \cos(lat_2) \times \cos(lon_2 - lon_1)\right] \times R$$

This formula determines the cosine between the two positions; the angle with that cosine is multiplied by the radius of the earth, R, to get the distance along the surface. We can use R = 3,440 NM, R = 3,959 mi, or R = 6,371 km; we get reasonably accurate distances in nautical miles, statute miles, or kilometers.

This formula doesn't work well with small distances. The haversine formula is preferred to compute distances more accurately. Here is some background information `http://en.wikipedia.org/wiki/Haversine_formula`.

According to the OED, the term "haversine" was coined in 1835 by Prof. James Inman. The term refers to the way the sine function is used.

The haversine calculation is often shown as a sequence of five steps:

1. $\Delta lat = lat_2 - lat_1$

2. $\Delta lon = lon_2 - lon_1$

3. $a = \sin^2\left(\dfrac{\Delta lat}{2}\right) + \cos\left(lat_1\right) \times \cos\left(lat_2\right) \times \sin^2\left(\dfrac{\Delta lon}{2}\right)$

4. $c = 2\arcsin\sqrt{a}$

5. $d = R \times a$

The required sine, cosine, and square root portions of this are part of Python's `math` library. When we look at the definitions of sine and cosine, we see that they work in radians. We'll need to convert our latitude and longitude values from degrees to radians. The rule is simple ($\left(2\pi r = \dfrac{d}{360}\right)$), but the `math` library includes a function, `radians()`, which will do this for us.

We can look at `http://rosettacode.org/wiki/Haversine_formula#Python` to learn from the example already there.

We'll use this as the distance between two points:

```
from math import radians, sin, cos, sqrt, asin

MI= 3959
NM= 3440
KM= 6371

def haversine( point1, point2, R=MI ):
    """Distance between points.
    point1 and point2 are two-tuples of latitude and longitude.
    R is radius, R=MI computes in miles.
    """
    lat_1, lon_1 = point1
    lat_2, lon_2 = point2

    Δ_lat = radians(lat_2 - lat_1)
    Δ_lon = radians(lon_2 - lon_1)
    lat_1 = radians(lat_1)
    lat_2 = radians(lat_2)

    a = sin(Δ_lat/2)**2 + cos(lat_1)*cos(lat_2)*sin(Δ_lon/2)**2
    c = 2*asin(sqrt(a))

    return R * c
```

We've imported the five functions from the `math` library that we require for this calculation.

We've defined three constants with the earth's radius in various units. We can plug any of these into our `haversine()` function as the R parameter to compute distances in different units. These values are approximations, but they'll work to determine how far apart two points are. We can plug in more accurate values if we want more precise answers. Since the earth isn't perfectly spherical, we have to be sure to use mean radius values.

The `haversine()` function will accept two required positional parameters and an optional parameter. The two positional parameters will be two-tuples of latitude and longitude. We'd like to use a syntax like `(36.12, -86.67)` to keep the two coordinates bound in a single Python value. The R parameter is optional because we've provided a default value for it. We can use this function to get distances in kilometers instead of in miles: `haversine( (36.12, -86.67), (33.94, -118.40), R=KM)`.

The body of our function breaks down the two-tuples into their component latitude and longitude values. We compute the `Δ_lat` variable by subtracting and converting the result to radians. Similarly, we compute the `Δ_lon` variable by subtracting and converting the result to radians. And yes variable names which begin with the Greek Δ character are perfectly valid in Python. After this, we can also convert the other two latitudes to radians. We can then plug these values to other formulae to compute a, c, and finally the distance.

We have a test case based on the example from the Rosetta Code website:

```
>>> from ch_4_ex_3 import haversine
>>> round(haversine((36.12, -86.67), (33.94, -118.40), R=6372.8), 5)
2887.25995
```

Note that we rounded the answer to five decimal places. Floating-point numbers are an approximation; it's possible to see some variations between hardware and OS in precisely how floating-point numbers work. By limiting ourselves to five decimal places, we're confident that variations in hardware won't upset the test case.

We can use this `haversine()` function with our geocode results to compute distances between locations; this will help us find the closest locations.

Combining geocoding and haversine

Between geocoding and the `haversine()` function, we have the tools to compute the approximate distance between addresses.

Let's take 333 Waterside, Norfolk, Virginia, as our current base of operations. Let's say our informant wants to meet either at 456 Granby or 111 W Tazewell. Which one is closer?

First, we'll need to clean up our geocoding script to make it a usable function. Rather than simply printing a result, we'll need to get the values out of the results dictionary to make a sequence of the two-tuples of the latitude and longitude responses.

Here's what we'll need to add:

```
def geocode( address ):
...   The previous processing ...
loc_dict= [r['geometry']['location'] for r in response['results']]
loc_pairs= [(l['lat'],l['lng']) for l in loc_dict]
return loc_pairs
```

We've used two generator expressions to dismantle the results. The first generator expression took the location information from each alternative in the `response['results']` sequence. For geocoding, there should only be one expression, but it's simpler if we pretend we'll get multiple responses.

The second generator expression turned the `'lat'` and `'lng'` elements of the location dictionary into a two-tuple. Having latitude and longitude two-tuples will play well with our `havesine()` function.

Here's how we can get three latitude-longitude pairs:

```
base = geocode( "333 Waterside, Norfolk, VA, 23510" )[0]
loc1 = geocode( "456 Granby St, Norfolk, VA" )[0]
loc2 = geocode( "111 W Tazewell, Norfolk, VA" )[0]
```

We've applied our `geocode()` function to get a list of two-tuples and then used `[0]` to pick the first element from each response list.

Here's how we can report the distances from the base to each location:

```
print("Base", base)
print("Loc1", loc1, haversine(base, loc1))
print("Loc2", loc2, haversine(base, loc2))
```

We applied our `haversine()` function to compute distances. By default, the distances are in miles, not that the units matter to carry out a relative comparison of closer versus further away.

Here are the results:

```
Base (36.8443027, -76.2910835)
Loc1 (36.8525159, -76.2890381) 0.578671972401055
Loc2 (36.8493341, -76.291527) 0.3485214316218753
```

We can see that the second location (Loc2), the Tazewell address, is much closer to our base than the Granby street address.

Also, we can see that we need to format these numbers to make them look better. Since we're only working with an approximate mean earth radius in miles, most of those decimal places are just visual noise.

Compressing data to make grid codes

Latitudes and longitudes are bulky to transmit. They have a lot of digits and some peculiar punctuation. Over the years, some alternatives have risen that abbreviate a location using a simpler notation. The essential idea is to convert latitude and longitude numbers from their degree-minute-second numbers into a sequence of letters and digits that represent the same information.

We'll look at three compression schemes: the GeoRef system, the Maindenhead Locator, and NAC. Each of these encodings involves doing some arithmetic calculations to convert numbers from decimal (base 10) to another base. We'll also use a number of string operations to translate numbers to characters and characters to numbers.

Another interesting programming issue is that these encodings don't work directly with latitudes and longitudes. The problem with simply using latitudes and longitudes is that they're signed numbers: -90 (S) to +90 (N) and -180 (W) to +180 (E). Also, longitudes have a bigger range (360 values), whereas latitudes have a smaller range (180 values). To simplify the encoding, we'll apply a common programming hack: we'll offset and scale the values. We'll see a number of ways to apply this clever technique.

In effect, the scaling and offsetting moves the map's (0, 0) origin to somewhere in Antarctica: at the south pole and right on 180° longitude. The center of these grid maps is somewhere off the coast of West Africa, and the upper-right corner will wind up in the Bering Sea, right at the north pole and next to the 180° longitude.

Creating GeoRef codes

The GeoRef system compresses a latitude-longitude position using four letters and as many as eight digits. This system can also be used to encode descriptions of regions as well as altitudes. We'll stick with locations on the surface.

For some background information, see http://en.wikipedia.org/wiki/Georef.

This system encodes decimal numbers using 24-letter codes chosen from A to Z, omitting I and O. This means that we can't simply rely on a handy copy of the alphabet such as `string.ascii_uppercase` to provide the letter codes. We'll have to define our own GeoRef letters. We can compute the letters with an expression as follows:

```
>>> string.ascii_uppercase.replace("O","").replace("I","")
'ABCDEFGHJKLMNPQRSTUVWXYZ'
```

The GeoRef codes slice the world map into a 12 x 24 grid of 15° x 15° quadrangles. The latitude is measured in positive numbers from the South Pole. The longitude is measured in positive numbers from the International Date Line. When we divide 180° of latitude into 15° steps, we can encode a part of this three-digit number using 12 letters from A to M (omitting I). When we divide 360° of longitude into 15° steps, we can encode a part of this three-digit number using 24 letters from A to Z (omitting I and O).

We can then divide each 15° quadrangles into 15 bands using letters A to Q (again, skipping I and O). This creates a four- character code for the entire degrees portion of a latitude and longitude position.

If we had a latitude of 38°17'10"N, we'd offset this to be 128° north of the south pole and divide it by 15°:

```
>>> divmod(38+90,15)
(8, 8)
```

These values are encoded as J and J.

A longitude of 76°24'42"W is encoded as shown in the following code. This is -76.41167°, which we offset by 180° before using `divmod` to calculate the two characters:

```
>>> divmod( -76+180, 15 )
(6, 14)
```

This gives us letters G and P. We interleave longitude and latitude characters so that the whole string is GJPJ. We've encoded six digits of latitude and longitude into four characters.

The leftover minutes and seconds can be encoded as two, three, or four digits. For the latitude, 17'10" can be encoded as 17.16 minutes. This is 17, an intermediate 171, or a detailed 1716.

Here's the entire encoder the for GeoRef codes:

```
def ll_2_georef( lat, lon ):
    f_lat, f_lon = lat+90, lon+180
    lat_0, lat_1 = divmod( int(f_lat), 15 )
    lon_0, lon_1 = divmod( int(f_lon), 15 )
    lat_m, lon_m = 6000*(f_lat-int(f_lat)), 6000*(f_lon-int(f_lon))
    return "{lon_0}{lat_0}{lon_1}{lat_1}{lon_m:04d}{lat_m:04d}".
format(
        lon_0= georef_uppercase[lon_0],
        lat_0= georef_uppercase[lat_0],
        lon_1= georef_uppercase[lon_1],
        lat_1= georef_uppercase[lat_1],
        lon_m= int(lon_m),
        lat_m= int(lat_m),
    )
```

We offset the latitudes and longitudes so that we don't have to deal with signed numbers. We used the `divmod()` function to divide by 15° and get both a quotient and a remainder. We can then use our `georef_uppercase` letters to translate the numeric quotients and remainders into expected character codes.

The fractional values, for example, `f_lat-int(f_lat)`, are scaled by 6000 to create a number between 0000 and 5999, which is simply the number of minutes in 100ths.

We've used the string `format()` method to assemble the four-character codes and four-digit numeric codes into a single string. The first two letters are longitude and latitude to provide a position to the nearest 15°. The next two letters have more longitude and latitude details to refine this to the nearest 1°. The digits are in two blocks of four to provide the detailed minutes.

Here's a more complete example of the output. We'll encode 36°50.63'N 076°17.49'W:

```
lat, lon = 36+50.63/60, -(76+17.49/60)
print(lat, lon)
print(ll_2_georef(lat, lon))
```

We've converted degrees and minutes to degrees. Then, we applied our GeoRef conversion to the values in degrees. Here's what the output looks like:

```
36.843833333333336 -76.2915
GJPG42515063
```

The code `GJPG` is an approximation of the given location; it could be off by almost 80 nautical miles at the equator. The error gets smaller toward the poles. The code `GJPG4250` uses the two-digit encoding of whole minutes to get within a few miles of the coordinates.

Decoding a GeoRef code

When we decode a GeoRef code, we have to separate the two parts: the four characters at the beginning and the numeric details at the end. Once we've split off the first four characters, we can divide the number of remaining characters in half. One half of the digits will be longitude and the rest will be latitude.

The first four characters must be looked up in our special GeoRef alphabet. We'll find each character's position in the ABCDEFGHJKLMNPQRSTUVWXYZ string to get a numeric value. An expression such as georef_uppercase.find('Q') gives us 14: the position of Q in that alphabet. We can then multiply one position by 15° and add the other position number to translate two characters to the degrees portion of GeoRef.

The remaining digits are simply minutes, which are 1/60 of a degree. During conversion there is a matter of creating a number and possibly dividing it by 10 or 100. The final step is to take out the offsets that were used to avoid signed arithmetic.

The whole thing looks like this:

```
def georef_2_ll( grid ):
    lon_0, lat_0, lon_1, lat_1= grid[:4]
    rest= grid[4:]
    pos= len(rest)//2
    if pos:
        scale= { 4: 100, 3: 10, 2: 1 }[pos]
        lon_frac, lat_frac = float(rest[:pos])/scale,
float(rest[pos:])/scale
    else:
        lon_frac, lat_frac = 0, 0
    lat= georef_uppercase.find(lat_0)*15+georef_uppercase.
find(lat_1)+lat_frac/60
    lon= georef_uppercase.find(lon_0)*15+georef_uppercase.
find(lon_1)+lon_frac/60
    return lat-90, lon-180
```

This works by separating the first four positions of the code into four longitude and latitude characters. Note that the positions are interleaved: longitude first, latitude second.

The rest of the string is divided in half. If there are any characters in the second half, then the first half (two, three, or four characters) will be longitude minutes; the second half will be latitude minutes.

We've used a simple literal mapping from the length (two, three, or four) to the scaling values (1, 10, and 100). We defined a dictionary with the mapping from the position to scale factor and applied the number of positions, pos, to that dictionary. We could have done this using an arithmetic calculation, too: 10**(pos-1); this calculation also works to convert pos to a power of 10.

We will take the string of characters, convert them to float and then scale them to create a proper value for minutes. Here is an example of what the scaling looks like:

```
>>> float("5063")/100
50.63
```

The else condition handles the case where there are only four positions in the grid code. If this is true, then the letters are all we have and the minutes will be zero.

We can calculate the offset values using one letter scaled by 15°, the next letter scaled by 1°, and the minutes by the 60th of a degree. The final step, of course, is to remove the offsets to create the expected signed numbers.

Consider that we use this:

```
print( georef_2_ll( "GJPG425506" ) )
```

We'll see an output like this:

```
(36.843333333333334, -76.29166666666667)
```

We chopped the longer GeoRef down to a 10-digit code. This has two 3-digit encodings of the minutes. We have elected to lose some accuracy, but this can also simplify the transmission of secret information.

Creating Maidenhead grid codes

As compared to relatively simple grid codes covered previously, we have an alternative notation called the **Maidenhead system**. This is used by Ham radio operators to exchange information about the locations of their stations. Maidenhead is a town in England; the Maidenhead code is **IO91PM**.

For more information, see http://en.wikipedia.org/wiki/Maidenhead_Locator_System.

The Maidenhead algorithms involve somewhat more sophisticated math based on creating a base 240 representation of the latitude and longitude numbers. We can encode each *digit* of a base 240 number using a letter-digit combination. We'll show a common technique to convert a floating-point number to an integer using a series of steps.

The Maidenhead system slices the world map into a 180 × 180 grid of quadrangles; each quadrangle has 1° in the N-S direction and 2° in the E-W direction. We can encode these quadrangles using a base 240 numbering system where a letter and digit are used to denote each of the digits of the base 240 system. Since the grid is only 180×180, we don't need the full range of our base 240 numbers.

To specify a position more accurately, we can slice each cell of the grid into 240 x 240 smaller cells. This means that an eight-position code gets us within .25 nautical miles in the N-S direction and .5 nautical miles in the E-W direction. For Ham radio purposes, this may be sufficient. For our address-level geocoding, we'll need more accuracy.

We can apply the same letter-number operation a third time, dividing each tiny rectangle into 240 even smaller pieces. This gets us more than the accuracy we need.

We are creating a three-digit number in a 240-number system where each base 240 digit is represented by a letter-number pair. We're performing the following calculation to create the three digits $(x_0, x_1 x_2)$ that encode a number, n:

$$n = 360 \times \left(\frac{x_0 \times 240^2 + x_1 \times 240 + x_2}{240^3} \right)$$

Here's the whole process:

```
def ll_2_mh( lat, lon ):
    def let_num( v ):
        l, n = divmod( int(v), 10 )
        return string.ascii_uppercase[l], string.digits[n]
    f_lat= lat+90
    f_lon= (lon+180)/2
    y0, y1 = let_num( f_lat )
    x0, x1 = let_num( f_lon )
    f_lat= 240*(f_lat-int(f_lat))
    f_lon= 240*(f_lon-int(f_lon))
    y2, y3 = let_num( f_lat )
    x2, x3 = let_num( f_lon )
    f_lat= 240*(f_lat-int(f_lat))
    f_lon= 240*(f_lon-int(f_lon))
    y4, y5 = let_num( f_lat )
    x4, x5 = let_num( f_lon )
    return "".join( [
        x0, y0, x1, y1, x2, y2, x3, y3, x4, y4, x5, y5 ] )
```

We've defined an internal function, `let_num()`, inside our `ll_2_mh()` function. The internal `let_num()` function translates a number in the 0 to 240 range into a letter and a digit. It uses the `divmod()` function to decompose the number into a quotient from 0 to 24 and a remainder from 0 to 9. This function then uses these two numeric values as indices in the `string.ascii_uppercase` and `string.digits` strings to return two characters. Each letter-number pair is a representation for a single digit of the base 240 number system. Rather than invent 240-digit symbols, we've repurposed a letter-digit pair to write the 240 distinct values.

The first real step is to convert the raw, signed latitude and longitude to our maidenhead grid version. The `f_lat` variable is the original latitude with an offset of 90 to make it strictly positive, in the range 0 to 180. The `f_lon` variable is the original longitude offset by 180 and divided by 2 to make it strictly positive, in the range 0 to 180. We created the initial letter-number pairs from these initial values of degrees: `f_lat` and `f_lon`.

This works nicely for degrees. What about the fractions of a degree? Here's a common technique to work with representations of floating-point values.

If we use something like `lat-int(lat)`, we'll compute the fractional portion of the latitude. If we scale that by 240, we'll get a number that we can use with `divmod()` to get one of the 240-letter positions and a digit. The expression `240*(f_lat-int(f_lat))` will expand the fractional part of `f_lat` to a scale of 0 to 240. Here's an example of how this scaling works:

```
>>> f_lat= 36.84383
>>> 240*(f_lat-int(f_lat))
202.51919999999927
>>> 240*.84383
202.51919999999998
```

The original latitude is `36.84383`. The value of `f_lat-int(f_lat)` will be the fractional portion of that value, which is `.84383`. We multiply this by `240` to get the value, with an approximate result of `202.5192`.

We used the `let_num()` function to create a letter-and-digit pair. The remaining fractional value (`0.5192`) can be scaled again by 240 to get yet another letter-and-digit pair.

At this point, the details have reached the limit of relevance. 1/240/240 of a degree is about 6 feet. Most civilian GPS instruments are only accurate to about 16 feet.

The final step is to interleave longitude and latitude characters. We've done this by creating a list of characters in the desired order. The `string.join()` method uses the given string as a separator when assembling a list of strings. It's common to use `", ".join(some_list)` to create comma-separated items. We have used `"".join()` to assemble the final string with no separator characters.

Here's a more complete example of the output. We'll encode 36°50.63'N 076°17.49'W:

```
lat, lon = 36+50.63/60, -(76+17.49/60)
print( lat, lon )
print( ll_2_mh( lat, lon ) )
```

We converted degrees and minutes to degrees. Then, we applied our Maidenhead conversion to the values in degrees. The output looks like this:

```
36.843833333333336 -76.28333333333333
FM16UU52AM44
```

We can use portions of this to encode with varying degrees of accuracy. `FM16` is pretty coarse, whereas `FM16UU` is more accurate.

Decoding the Maidenhead grid codes

To decode the Maidenhead codes, we need to reverse the procedure we used to create the codes from latitudes and longitudes. We'll need to take all the even positions as a sequence of digits to create the longitude and all the odd positions as a sequence of digits to create the latitude. By looking up against `string.ascii_uppercase` and `string.digits`, we can transform characters into numbers.

Once we have a sequence of numbers, we can apply a sequence of weighing factors and add up the results. The whole thing looks like this:

```
def mh_2_ll( grid ):
    lon= grid[0::2] # even positions
    lat= grid[1::2] # odd positions
    assert len(lon) == len(lat)
    # Lookups will alternate letters and digits
    decode = [ string.ascii_uppercase, string.digits,
            string.ascii_uppercase, string.digits,
            string.ascii_uppercase, string.digits,
            ]
    lons= [ lookup.find(char.upper()) for char, lookup in zip( lon,
decode ) ]
    lats= [ lookup.find(char.upper()) for char, lookup in zip( lat,
decode ) ]
```

```
weights = [ 10.0, 1.0,
            1/24, 1/240,
            1/240/24, 1/240/240, ]
lon = sum( w*d for w,d in zip(lons, weights) )
lat = sum( w*d for w,d in zip(lats, weights) )
return lat-90, 2*lon-180
```

We used Python's very elegant slice notation to take the string apart into even and odd positions. The expression `grid[0::2]` specifies a slice of the `grid` string. The `[0::2]` slice starts at position `0`, extends to the very end, and increments by 2. The `[1::2]` slice starts at position `1`, extends to the very end, and also increments by 2.

The `decode` list contains six strings that will be used to translate each character into a numeric value. The first character will be found in `string.ascii_uppercase` and the second character will be found in `string.digits`. The positions at which the characters are found in these strings will become the numeric values that we can use to compute latitudes and longitudes.

For example, the value of `'ABCDEFGHIJKLMNOPQRSTUVWXYZ'.find('M')` is 12.

We've used a generator expression and the `zip()` function to do the real work of the translation. The `zip()` function will produce a sequence of pairs; each pair will have one character chosen from the input grid code and one lookup string chosen from the `decode` lists. We can then use `lookup.find(char.upper())` to locate the given character in the given lookup string. The result will be a sequence of integer positions.

Once we have a sequence of the numeric values, we can apply the sequence of weightings to convert each position to a degree or a fraction of a degree. Again, we used `zip()` to create two-tuples from the digits and the weights. The generator then multiplied the numeric value by the weight. The built-in `sum()` function created the final value from the numbers and weights.

For example, we might have a value in the `lons` variable of `[5, 1, 20, 6, 0, 0]`. The weights are `[10.0, 1.0, 0.0416, 0.00416, 0.00017361, 1.7361e-05]`. When we use `zip()` to zip these two sequences, we'll get pairs like this:

```
[(5, 10.0), (1, 1.0), (20, 0.0416),
(6, 0.00416), (0, 0.00017361),
(0, 1.7361e-05)]
```

The products look like this:

```
[50.0, 1.0, 0.832, 0.02495999999999996, 0.0, 0.0]
```

The sum is `51.85696`.

The final step is to undo the offsets we used to force the latitudes to be positive and the longitudes to have values between 0 and 180 instead of -180 to +180. The intermediate longitude result `51.85696` becomes `-76.28608`.

Consider that we evaluate this:

```
print( mh_2_ll( "FM16UU62" ) )
```

We get the following decoded positions:

```
(36.84166666666667, -76.28333333333333)
```

This nicely decodes the values we encoded in the previous section.

Creating natural area codes

The **Natural Area Code (NAC)** is yet another way to encode geographic position information into a short character string. The whole NAC system can include altitude information along with the surface position. We'll focus on the latitude and longitude conversions for NAC.

See `http://www.nacgeo.com/nacsite/documents/nac.asp`, for more information

This uses base 30 instead of base 240; we can use most of the alphabets plus some digits to represent a single base 30 digit. This implementation will show a different approach to convert floating-point numbers to an integer approximation. This will combine multiple calculation steps into longer expressions.

NAC uses a 30-character encoding that employs digits and consonants. The string used for encoding and decoding is this:

```
>>> nac_uppercase= "0123456789BCDFGHJKLMNPQRSTVWXZ"
>>> len(nac_uppercase)
30
>>> nac_uppercase[10]
'B'
>>> nac_uppercase.find('B')
10
```

We can take a longitude (-180 to +180), and add an offset to put it in the range of 0 to 360. If we scale this by `(30**4)/360`, we'll get a number in the range 0 to 810000. This can be converted to a four-digit base 30 number.

Similarly, we can take a latitude (-90 to +90), and add an offset to put it in the range of 0 to 180. If we scale this by $(30**4)/180$, similarly, we'll get a number that can be converted to a four-digit base 30 number. The big win here is that we've replaced long strings of base 10 digits with shorter strings of base 30 digits.

The suggested algorithm to encode this is:

```
def ll_2_nac( lat, lon ):
    f_lon= (lon+180)/360
    x0 = int(    f_lon*30)
    x1 = int((   f_lon*30-x0)*30)
    x2 = int(((  f_lon*30-x0)*30-x1)*30)
    x3 = int(.5+(((f_lon*30-x0)*30-x1)*30-x2)*30)

    f_lat= (lat+90)/180
    y0 = int(    f_lat*30 )
    y1 = int((   f_lat*30-y0)*30)
    y2 = int(((  f_lat*30-y0)*30-y1)*30)
    y3 = int(0.5+(((f_lat*30-y0)*30-y1)*30-y2)*30)

    print( x0, x1, x2, x3, y0, y1, y2, y3 )
    return "".join( [
        nac_uppercase[x0], nac_uppercase[x1],
        nac_uppercase[x2], nac_uppercase[x3],
        " ",
        nac_uppercase[y0], nac_uppercase[y1],
        nac_uppercase[y2], nac_uppercase[y3],
    ])
```

We've scaled the longitude by adding an offset and dividing it by 360. This creates a number between `0` and `1.0`. We can then encode this into base 30 using a large number of multiplications and subtractions. There are a number of ways to optimize this.

Each step follows a similar pattern. We'll step through the longitude calculation. Here's the first character calculation:

```
>>> lon= -151.3947
>>> f_lon= (lon+180)/360
>>> f_lon
0.07945916666666666
>>> x0 = int(f_lon*30)
>>> x0
2
```

The first step computes f_lon, the fraction of 360 for this longitude (151.3947W). When we multiply f_lon by 30, we get 2.383775. The integer portion, 2, will become the first character. The fraction will be encoded in the remaining three characters.

Here's the next character, based on the first:

```
>>> x1 = int((f_lon*30-x0)*30)
>>> x1
11
```

The calculation of (f_lon*30-x0) computes the fraction, .383775. We then scale this by 30 to get 11.51325. The integer portion, 11, will become the second character. The fraction will be encoded in the remaining two characters.

At each step, we take all of the previous digits to compute the remaining fractional components. Here are the last two characters:

```
>>> x2 = int((( f_lon*30-x0)*30-x1)*30)
>>> x2
15
>>> x3 = int(0.5+(((f_lon*30-x0)*30-x1)*30-x2)*30)
>>> x3
12
```

Each of these character, takes the difference between the original number (f_lon) and the previously computed digits to get the remaining fraction. The final step involves a lot of multiplication. Previously, in the *Creating Maidenhead grid codes* section, we showed a variation on this theme that didn't use quite so many multiplication operations.

As an example, we may perform the following:

```
lat, lon = 43.6508, -151.3947
print( ll_2_nac( lat, lon ) )
```

The output of this is:

```
2CHD Q87M
```

This is a pretty tidy summary of a latitude and longitude.

Decoding natural area codes

Decoding natural area codes is actually a conversion from a base 30 number to a value between 0 and 810,000. This is then scaled into a proper latitude or longitude value. Although base 30 numbers don't seem simple, the programming is actually pretty succinct. Here's the suggested algorithm:

```
def nac_2_ll( grid ):
    X, Y = grid[:4], grid[5:]
    x = [nac_uppercase.find(c) for c in X]
    y = [nac_uppercase.find(c) for c in Y]
    lon = (x[0]/30+x[1]/30**2+x[2]/30**3+x[3]/30**4)*360-180
    lat = (y[0]/30+y[1]/30**2+y[2]/30**3+y[3]/30**4)*180-90
    return lat, lon
```

We've decomposed each part of the nine-character NAC grid code into a longitude substring and a latitude substring. We used a generator function to lookup each character in our `nac_uppercase` alphabet. This will map each character to a numeric position between 0 and 29.

Once we have the sequence of the four base 30 digits, we can compute a number from the digits. The following expression does the essential work:

```
(x[0]/30+x[1]/30**2+x[2]/30**3+x[3]/30**4)
```

The preceding expression is an optimization of the polynomial, $n = \frac{\left(x_o \times 30^3 + x_1 \times 30^2 x_2 \times 30^1 x_3 \times 30^0\right)}{30^4}$. The Python code simplifies the constants in each term — rather than computing `x[0]*30**3/30**4`; this is reduced to `x[0]/30`.

The intermediate results are scaled by 360 or 180 and offset to get the expected signed values for the final result.

Consider that we evaluate the following:

```
print( nac_2_ll( "2CHD Q87M" ) )
```

We get the following as a result:

```
(43.650888888888886, -151.39466666666667)
```

This shows how we decode an NAC to recover the latitude and longitude of a position.

Solving problems – closest good restaurant

We want to meet our secret informant at a good restaurant that's a reasonable distance from our base. In order to locate a good restaurant, we need to gather some additional information. In this case, good means a passing grade from the health inspectors.

Before we can even have a meeting, we'll need to use basic espionage skills to locate the health code survey results for local restaurants.

We'll create a Python application to combine many things to sort through the results. We'll perform the following steps:

1. We'll start with the restaurant health score information.

2. We need to geocode the restaurant addresses if it hasn't been done already. In some cases, geocoding is done for us. In other cases, we'll be using a web service for this.

3. We need to filter and organize restaurants by good scores. We'll also need to use our `haversine()` function to compute the distance from our base.

4. Finally, we need to communicate this to our network, ideally using a short NAC code embedded within an image that we post to a social media site. See *Chapter 3, Encoding Secret Messages with Steganography*, for details on this final step.

In many cities, the health code data is available online. A careful search will reveal a useful dataset. In other cities, the health inspection data isn't readily available online. We might have to dig considerably deep to track down even a few restaurants near our base of operations.

Some cities use **Yelp** to publicize restaurant health code inspection data. We can read about the YELP API to search for restaurants on the following link:

`http://www.yelp.com/developers/documentation`

We might also find some useful data on InfoChimps at `http://www.infochimps.com/tags/restaurant`.

One complexity we often encounter is the use of HTML-based APIs for this kind of information. This is not intentional obfuscation, but the use of HTML complicates analysis of the data. Parsing HTML to extract meaningful information isn't easy; we'll need an extra library to handle this.

We'll look at two approaches: good, clean data and more complex HTML data parsing. In both cases, we need to create a Python object that acts as a container for a collection of attributes. First, we'll divert to look at the `SimpleNamespace` class. Then, we'll use this to collect information.

Creating simple Python objects

We have a wide variety of ways to define our own Python objects. We can use the central built-in types such as dict to define an object that has a collection of attribute values. When looking at information for a restaurant, we could use something like this:

```
some_place = { 'name': 'Secret Base', 'address': '333 Waterside Drive'
}
```

Since this is a mutable object, we can add attribute values and change the values of the existing attributes. The syntax is a bit *clunky*, though. Here's what an update to this object looks like:

```
some_place['lat']= 36.844305
some_place['lng']= -76.29112
```

The extra `[]` brackets and `''` characters seem needless. We'd like to have a notation that's a little cleaner than this very general key-value syntax used for dictionaries.

One common solution is to use a proper class definition. The syntax looks like this:

```
class Restaurant:
    def __init__(self, name, address):
        self.name= name
        self.address= address
```

We've defined a class with an initialization method, `__init__()`. The name of the initialization method is special, and only this name can be used. When the object is built, the initialization method is evaluated to assign initial values to the attributes of the object.

This allows us to create an object more succinctly:

```
some_place= Restaurant( name='Secret Base', address='333 Waterside
Drive' )
```

We've used explicit keyword arguments. The use of `name=` and `address=` isn't *required*. However, as class definitions become more complex, it's often more flexible and more clear to use keyword argument values.

We can update the object nicely too, as follows:

```
some_place.lat= 36.844305
some_place.lng= -76.29112
```

This works out best when we have a lot of unique processing that is bound to each object. In this case, we don't actually have any processing to associate with the attributes; we just want to collect those attributes in a tidy capsule. The formal class definition is too much overhead for such a simple problem.

Python also gives us a very flexible structure called a **namespace**. This is a mutable object that we can access using simple attribute names, as shown in the following code:

```
from types import SimpleNamespace
some_place= SimpleNamespace( name='Secret Base', address='333
Waterside Drive' )
```

The syntax to create a namespace *must* use keyword arguments (name='The Name'). Once we've created this object, we can update it using a pleasant attribute access, as shown in the following snippet:

```
some_place.lat= 36.844305
some_place.lng= -76.29112
```

The SimpleNamespace class gives us a way to build an object that contains a number of individual attribute values.

We can also create a namespace from a dictionary using Python's ** notation. Here's an example:

```
>>> SimpleNamespace( **{'name': 'Secret Base', 'address': '333
Waterside Drive'} )
namespace(address='333 Waterside Drive', name='Secret Base')
```

The ** notation tells Python that a dictionary object contains keyword arguments for the function. The dictionary keys are the parameter names. This allows us to build a dictionary object and then use it as the arguments to a function.

Recall that JSON tends to encode complex data structures as a dictionary. Using this ** technique, we can transform a JSON dictionary into SimpleNamespace, and replace the clunky object['key'] notation with a cleaner object.key notation.

Working with HTML web services – tools

In some cases, the data we want is tied up in HTML websites. The City of Norfolk, for example, relies on the State of Virginia's VDH health portal to store its restaurant health code inspection data.

In order to make sense of the intelligence encoded in the HTML notation on the WWW, we need to be able to parse the HTML markup that surrounds the data. Our job is greatly simplified by the use of special higher-powered weaponry; in this case, BeautifulSoup.

Start with `https://pypi.python.org/pypi/beautifulsoup4/4.3.2` or `http://www.crummy.com/software/BeautifulSoup/`.

If we have Easy Install (or PIP), we can use these tools to install BeautifulSoup. Back in *Chapter 1, Our Espionage Toolkit*, we should have installed one (or both) of these tools to install more tools.

We can use Easy Install to install BeautifulSoup like this:

```
sudo easy_install-3.3 beautifulsoup4
```

Mac OS X and GNU/Linux users will need to use the `sudo` command. Windows users won't use the `sudo` command.

Once we have BeautifulSoup, we can use it to parse the HTML code looking for specific facts buried in an otherwise cryptic jumble of HTML tags.

Before we can go on, you'll need to read the quickstart documentation and bring yourself up to speed on BeautifulSoup. Once you've done that, we'll move to extracting data from HTML web pages.

Start with `http://www.crummy.com/software/BeautifulSoup/bs4/doc/#quick-start`.

An alternative tool is **scrapy**. For information see `http://scrapy.org`. Also, read *Instant Scrapy Web Mining and Scraping, Travis Briggs, Packt Publishing*, for details on using this tool. Unfortunately, as of this writing, scrapy is focused on Python 2, not Python 3.

Working with HTML web services – getting the page

In the case of VDH health data for the City of Norfolk, the HTML scraping is reasonably simple. We can leverage the strengths of BeautifulSoup to dig into the HTML page very nicely.

Once we've created a BeautifulSoup object from the HTML page, we will have an elegant technique to navigate down through the hierarchy of the HTML tags. Each HTML tag name (`html`, `body`, and so on) is also a BeautifulSoup query that locates the first instance of that tag.

An expression such as soup.html.body.table can locate the first <table> in the HTML <body> tag. In the case of the VDH restaurant data, that's precisely the data we want.

Once we've found the table, we need to extract the rows. The HTML tag for each row is <tr> and we can use the BeautifulSoup table.find_all("tr") expression to locate all rows within a given <table> tag. Each tag's text is an attribute, .text. If the tag has attributes, we can treat the tag as if it's a dictionary to extract the attribute values.

We'll break down the processing of the VDH restaurant data into two parts: the web services query that builds Soup from HTML and the HTML parsing to gather restaurant information.

Here's the first part, which is getting the raw BeautifulSoup object:

```
scheme_host= "http://healthspace.com"
def get_food_list_by_name():
    path= "/Clients/VDH/Norfolk/Norolk_Website.nsf/Food-List-ByName"
    form = {
        "OpenView": "",
        "RestrictToCategory": "FAA4E68B1BBBB48F008D02BF09DD656F",
        "count": "400",
        "start": "1",
    }
    query= urllib.parse.urlencode( form )
    with urllib.request.urlopen(scheme_host + path + "?" + query) as data:
        soup= BeautifulSoup( data.read() )
    return soup
```

This repeats the web services queries we've seen before. We've separated three things here: the scheme_host string, the path string, and query. The reason for this is that our overall script will be using the scheme_host with other paths. And we'll be plugging in lots of different query data.

For this basic food_list_by_name query, we've built a form that will get 400 restaurant inspections. The RestrictToCategory field in the form has a magical key that we must provide to get the Norfolk restaurants. We found this via a basic web espionage technique: we poked around on the website and checked the URLs used when we clicked on each of the links. We also used the Developer mode of Safari to explore the page source.

In the long run, we want all of the inspections. To get started, we've limited ourselves to 400 so that we don't spend too long waiting to run a test of our script.

The response object was used by BeautifulSoup to create an internal representation of the web page. We assigned this to the `soup` variable and returned it as the result of the function.

In addition to returning the `soup` object, it can also be instructive to print it. It's quite a big pile of HTML. We'll need to parse this to get the interesting details away from the markup.

Working with HTML web services – parsing a table

Once we have a page of HTML information parsed into a BeautifulSoup object, we can examine the details of that page. Here's a function that will locate the table of restaurant inspection details buried inside the page.

We'll use a generator function to yield each individual row of the table, as shown in the following code:

```
def food_table_iter( soup ):
    """Columns are 'Name', '', 'Facility Location', 'Last Inspection',
    Plus an unnamed column with a RestrictToCategory key
    """
    table= soup.html.body.table
    for row in table.find_all("tr"):
        columns = [ td.text.strip() for td in row.find_all("td") ]
        for td in row.find_all("td"):
            if td.a:
                url= urllib.parse.urlparse( td.a["href"] )
                form= urllib.parse.parse_qs( url.query )
                columns.append( form['RestrictToCategory'][0] )
        yield columns
```

Notice that this function begins with a triple-quoted string. This is a *docstring* and it provides documentation about the function. Good Python style insists on a docstring in every function. The Python help system will display the docstrings for functions, modules, and classes. We've omitted them to save space. Here, we included it because the results of this particular iterator can be quite confusing.

This function requires a parsed Soup object. The function uses simple tag navigation to locate the first `<table>` tag in the HTML `<body>` tag. It then uses the table's `find_all()` method to locate all of the rows within that table.

For each row, there are two pieces of processing. First, a generator expression is used to find all the `<td>` tags within that row. Each `<td>` tag's text is stripped of excess white space and the collection forms a list of cell values. In some cases, this kind of processing is sufficient.

In this case, however, we also need to decode an HTML `<a>` tag, which has a reference to the details for a given restaurant. We use a second `find_all("td")` expression to examine each column again. Within each column, we check for the presence of an `<a>` tag using a simple `if td.a:` loop. If there is an `<a>` tag, we can get the value of the `href` attribute on that tag. When looking at the source HTML, this is the value inside the quotes of `<a href="">`.

This value of an HTML `href` attribute is a URL. We don't actually need the whole URL. We only need the query string within the URL. We've used the `urllib.parse.urlparse()` function to extract the various bits and pieces of the URL. The value of the `url.query` attribute is just the query string, after the `?`.

It turns out, we don't even want the entire query string; we only want the value for the key `RestrictToCategory`. We can parse the query string with `urllib.parse.parse_qs()` to get a form-like dictionary, which we assigned to the variable `form`. This function is the inverse of `urllib.parse.urlencode()`. The dictionary built by the `parse_qs()` function associates each key with a list of values. We only want the first value, so we use `form['RestrictToCategory'][0]` to get the key required for a restaurant.

Since this `food_table_iter ()` function is a generator, it must be used with a `for` statement or another generator function. We can use this function with a `for` statement as follows:

```
for row in  food_table_iter(get_food_list_by_name()):
    print(row)
```

This prints each row of data from the HTML table. It starts like this:

```
['Name', '', 'Facility Location', 'Last Inspection']
["Todd's Refresher", '', '150 W. Main St #100', '6-May-2014',
'43F6BE8576FFC376852574CF005E3FC0']
["'Chick-fil-A", '', '1205 N Military Highway', '13-Jun-2014',
'5BDECD68B879FA8C8525784E005B9926']
```

This goes on for 400 locations.

The results are unsatisfying because each row is a flat list of attributes. The name is in `row[0]` and the address in `row[2]`. This kind of reference to columns by position can be obscure. It would be much nicer to have named attributes. If we convert the results to a `SimpleNamespace` object, we can then use the `row.name` and `row.address` syntax.

Making a simple Python object from columns of data

We really want to work with an object that has easy-to-remember attribute names and not a sequence of anonymous column names. Here's a generator function that will build a `SimpleNamespace` object from a sequence of values produced by a function such as the `food_table_iter()` function:

```
def food_row_iter( table_iter ):
    heading= next(table_iter)
    assert ['Name', '', 'Facility Location', 'Last Inspection'] ==
heading
    for row in table_iter:
        yield SimpleNamespace(
            name= row[0], address= row[2], last_inspection= row[3],
            category= row[4]
        )
```

This function's argument must be an iterator like `food_table_iter(get_food_list_by_name())`. The function uses `next(table_iter)` to grab the first row, since that's only going to be a bunch of column titles. We'll assert that the column titles really are the standard column titles in the VDH data. If the assertion ever fails, it's a hint that VDH web data has changed.

For every row after the first row, we build a `SimpleNamespace` object by taking the specific columns from each row and assigning them nice names.

We can use this function as follows:

```
soup= get_food_list_by_name()
raw_columns=  food_table_iter(soup)
for business in food_row_iter( raw_column ):
    print( business.name, business.address )
```

The processing can now use nice attribute names, for example, `business.name`, to refer to the data we extracted from the HTML page. This makes the rest of the programming meaningful and clear.

What's also important is that we've combined two generator functions. The `food_table_iter()` function will yield small lists built from HTML table rows. The `food_row_iter()` function expects a sequence of lists that can be iterated, and will build `SimpleNamespace` objects from that sequence of lists. This defines a kind of composite processing pipeline built from smaller steps. Each row of the HTML table that starts in `food_table_iter()` is touched by `food_row_iter()` and winds up being processed by the `print()` function.

Enriching Python objects with geocodes

The Norfolk data we've gotten so far is only a list of restaurants. We still neither have inspection scores, nor do we have useful geocodes. We need to add these details to each business that we found in the initial list. This means making two more RESTful web services requests for each individual business.

The geocoding is relatively easy. We can use a simple request and update the `SimpleNamespace` object that we're using to model each business. The function looks like this:

```
def geocode_detail( business ):
    scheme_netloc_path = "https://maps.googleapis.com/maps/api/
geocode/json"
    form = {
        "address": business.address + ", Norfolk, VA",
        "sensor": "false",
        #"key": An API Key, if you signed up for one,
    }
    query = urllib.parse.urlencode( form, safe="," )
    with urllib.request.urlopen( scheme_netloc_path+"?"+query ) as
geocode:
        response= json.loads( geocode.read().decode("UTF-8") )
    lat_lon = response['results'][0]['geometry']['location']
    business.latitude= lat_lon['lat']
    business.longitude= lat_lon['lng']
    return business
```

We're using the Google geocoding API that we used earlier. We've made a few modifications. First, the data in the `form` variable has the `business.address` attribute from the `SimpleNamespace` object. We've had to add the city and state information, since that's not provided in the VDH address.

As with previous examples, we took only the first location of the response list with `response['results'][0]['geometry']['location']`, which is a small dictionary object with two keys: `lat` and `lon`. We've updated the namespace that represents our business by setting two more attributes, `business.latitude` and `business.longitude` from the values in this small dictionary.

The namespace object is mutable, so this function will update the object referred to by the variable `business`. We also returned the object. The `return` statement is not necessary, but sometimes it's handy because it allows us to create a fluent API for a sequence of functions.

Enriching Python objects with health scores

The bad news is that getting health scoring details requires yet more HTML parsing. The good news is that the details are placed in an easy-to-locate HTML `<table>` tag. We'll break this process into two functions: a web service request to get the BeautifulSoup object and more HTML parsing to explore that Soup.

Here's the URL request. This requires the category key that we parsed from the `<a>` tag in the `food_table_iter()` function shown previously:

```
def get_food_facility_history( category_key ):
    url_detail= "/Clients/VDH/Norfolk/Norolk_Website.nsf/Food-
FacilityHistory"
    form = {
        "OpenView": "",
        "RestrictToCategory": category_key
    }
    query= urllib.parse.urlencode( form )
    with urllib.request.urlopen(scheme_host + url_detail + "?" +
query) as data:
        soup= BeautifulSoup( data.read() )
    return soup
```

This request, like other HTML requests, builds a query string, opens the URL response object, and parses it to create a `BeautifulSoup` object. We're only interested in the `soup` instance. We return this value for use with HTML processing.

Also, note that part of the path, `Norolk_Website.nsf`, has a spelling error. Secret agents in the field are responsible for finding information in spite of these kind of problems.

We'll use this in a function that updates the `SimpleNamespace` object that we're using to model each business. The data extraction function looks like this:

```
def inspection_detail( business ):
    soup= get_food_facility_history( business.category )
    business.name2= soup.body.h2.text.strip()
    table= soup.body.table
    for row in table.find_all("tr"):
        column = list( row.find_all( "td" ) )
        name= column[0].text.strip()
        value= column[1].text.strip()
        setattr( business, vdh_detail_translate[name], value )
    return business
```

This function gets the `BeautifulSoup` object for a specific business. Given that Soup, it navigates to the first `<h2>` tag within the `<body>` tag. This should repeat the business name. We've updated the `business` object with this second copy of the name.

This function also navigates to the first `<table>` tag within the `<body>` tag via the `soup.body.table` expression. The HTML table has two columns: the left column contains a label and the right column contains the value.

To parse this kind of table, we stepped through each row using `table.find_all("tr")`. For each row, we built a list from `row.find_all( "td" )`. The first item in this list is the `<td>` tag that contains a name. The second item is the `<td>` tag that contains a value.

We can use a dictionary, `vdh_detail_translate`, to translate the names in the left column to a better looking Python attribute name, as shown in the following code:

```
vdh_detail_translate = {
    'Phone Number:': 'phone_number',
    'Facility Type:': 'facility_type',
    '# of Priority Foundation Items on Last Inspection:':
        'priority_foundation_items',
    '# of Priority Items on Last Inspection:': 'priority_items',
    '# of Core Items on Last Inspection:': 'core_items',
    '# of Critical Violations on Last Inspection:': 'critical_items',
    '# of Non-Critical Violations on Last Inspection:': 'non_critical_
items',
}
```

Using a dictionary like this allows us to use the expression `vdh_detail_translate[name]` to locate a pleasant attribute name (such as `core_item`) instead of the long string that's displayed in the original HTML.

We need to look closely at the use of the `setattr()` function that's used to update the `business` namespace:

```
setattr( business, vdh_detail_translate[name], value )
```

In other functions, we've used a simple assignment statement such as `business.attribute= value` to set an attribute of the namespace object. Implicitly, the simple assignment statement actually means `setattr( business, 'attribute', value )`. We can think of `setattr(object, attribute_string, value)` as the reason why Python implements the simple `variable.attribute= value` assignment statement.

In this function, we can't use a simple assignment statement, because the attribute name is a string that's looked up via a translation. We can use the `setattr()` function to update the business object using the attribute name string computed from `vdh_detail_translate[name]`.

Combining the pieces and parts

We can now look at the real question: finding high-quality restaurants. We can build a composite function that combines our previous functions. This can become a generator function that yields all of the details in a sequence of namespace objects, as shown in the following code:

```python
def choice_iter():
    base= SimpleNamespace( address= '333 Waterside Drive' )
    geocode_detail( base )
    print( base ) # latitude= 36.844305, longitude= -76.29111999999999
    )
    soup= get_food_list_by_name()
    for row in food_row_iter( food_table_iter( soup ) ):
        geocode_detail( row )
        inspection_detail( row )
        row.distance= haversine(
            (row.latitude, row.longitude),
            (base.latitude, base.longitude) )
        yield row
```

This will build a small object, `base`, to describe our base. The object will start with just the `address` attribute. After we apply the `geocode_detail()` function, it will also have a latitude and longitude.

The `print()` function will produce a line that looks like this:

```
namespace(address='333 Waterside Drive', latitude=36.844305,
longitude=-76.29111999999999)
```

The `get_food_list_by_name()` function will get a batch of restaurants. We use `food_table_iter()` to get the HTML table, and `food_row_iter()` to build individual `SimpleNamespace` objects from the HTML table. We then do some updates on each of those `SimpleNamespace` objects to provide restaurant inspection results and geocode information. We update the object yet again to add the distance from our base to the restaurant.

Finally, we yield the richly detailed namespace object that represents everything we need to know about a business.

Given this sequence of objects, we can apply some filters to exclude places over .75 miles away or with more than one problem reported:

```
for business in choice_iter():
    if business.distance > .75: continue
    if business.priority_foundation_items > 1: continue
    if business.priority_items > 1: continue
    if business.core_items > 1: continue
    print( business )
```

This script will apply four different filters to each response. If the business, for example, is too far away, the `continue` statement will end the processing of this item: the `for` statement will advance to the next. If the business has too many items, the `continue` statements will reject this business and advance to the next item. Only a business that passes all four tests will be printed.

Note that we've inefficiently processed each business through the `geocode_detail()` and `inspection_detail()` functions. A more efficient algorithm would apply the distance filter early in the processing. If we immediately reject places that are too far away, we will only need to get detailed restaurant health data for places that are close enough.

The important thing about this sequence of examples is that we integrated data from two different web services and folded them in our own value-added intelligence processing.

Working with clean data portals

A good example of a clean data portal is the City of Chicago. We can get the restaurant inspection data with a simple URL:

```
https://data.cityofchicago.org/api/views/4ijn-s7e5/rows.
json?accessType=DOWNLOAD
```

This will download all the restaurant inspection information in a tidy, easy-to-parse, JSON document. The only problem is the size. It has over 83,000 inspections and takes a very long time to download. If we apply a filter (for instance, only inspects done this year), we can cut the document down to a manageable size. More details on the various kinds of filters supported can be found at `http://dev.socrata.com/docs/queries.html`.

There's a lot of sophistication available. We'll define a simple filter based on the inspection date to limit ourselves to a subset of the available restaurant inspections.

A function to get the data looks like this:

```
def get_chicago_json():
    scheme_netloc_path= "https://data.cityofchicago.org/api/
views/4ijn-s7e5/rows.json"
    form = {
        "accessType": "DOWNLOAD",
        "$where": "inspection_date>2014-01-01",
    }
    query= urllib.parse.urlencode(form)
    with urllib.request.urlopen( scheme_netloc_path+"?"+query ) as
data:
        with open("chicago_data.json","w") as output:
            output.write( data.read() )
```

The `schem_netloc_path` variable includes two interesting details in path. `4ijn-s7e5` is the internal identity of the dataset we're looking for and `rows.json` specifies the format we want the data in.

The form we built includes a `$where` clause that will cut down on the volume of data to just the recent inspection reports. The Socrata API pages show us that we have a great deal of flexibility here.

As with other web services requests, we created a query and made the request using the `urllib.request.urlopen()` function. We opened an output file named `chicago_data.json` and wrote the document to that file for further processing. This saves us from having to retrieve the data repeatedly since it doesn't change too quickly.

We've done the processing via nested `with` statements to be assured that the files are closed and the network resources are properly released.

Making a simple Python object from a JSON document

The JSON document contains lots of individual dict objects. While a dict is a handy general-purpose structure, the syntax is a bit clunky. Having to use `object['some_key']` is awkward. It's nicer to work with `SimpleNamespace` objects and use pleasant attribute names. Using `object.some_key` is nicer.

Here's a function that will iterate through the massive JSON document with all of the inspection details:

```
def food_row_iter():
    with open( "chicago_data.json", encoding="UTF-8" ) as data_file:
        inspections = json.load( data_file )
```

```
headings = [item['fieldName']
    for item in inspections["meta"]["view"]["columns"] ]
print( headings )
for row in inspections["data"]:
    data= SimpleNamespace(
        **dict( zip( headings, row ) )
    )
    yield data
```

We've built a `SimpleNamespace` object from each individual row that was in the source data. The JSON document's data, in `inspections["data"]`, is a list of lists. It's rather hard to interpret because we need to know the position of each relevant field.

We created a list of headings based on the field names we found in `inspections["meta"]["view"]["columns"]`. The field names seem to all be valid Python variable names and will make good Python attribute names in a `SimpleNamespace` object.

Given this list of headings, we can then use the `zip()` function to interleave headings and data from each row that we find. This sequence of two-tuples can be used to create a dictionary by employing `dict( zip( headings, row ) )`. The dictionary can then be used to build the `SimpleNamespace` object.

The `**` syntax specifies that the items in the dictionary will become individual keyword parameters for `SimpleNamespace`. This will elegantly transform a dictionary such as `{'zip': '60608', 'results': 'Fail', 'city': 'CHICAGO', ... }` to a `SimpleNamespace` object as if we had written `SimpleNamespace( zip='60608', results='Fail', city='CHICAGO', ... )`.

Once we have a sequence of `SimpleNamespace` objects, we can do some minor updates to make them easier to work with. Here's a function that makes a few tweaks to each object:

```
def parse_details( business ):
    business.latitude= float(business.latitude)
    business.longitude= float(business.longitude)
    if business.violations is None:
        business.details = []
    else:
        business.details = [ v.strip() for v in business.violations.
split("|") ]
    return business
```

We've converted the longitude and latitude values from strings to float numbers. We need to do this in order to properly use the `haversine()` function to compute distance from our secret base. We've also split the `business.violations` value to a list of individual detailed violations. It's not clear what we'd do with this, but it might be helpful in understanding the `business.results` value.

Combining different pieces and parts

We can combine the processing into a function that's very similar to the `choice_iter()` function shown previously in the *Combining the pieces and parts* section. The idea is to create code that looks similar but starts with different source data.

This will iterate through the restaurant choices, depending on having `SimpleNamespace` objects that have been updated:

```
def choice_iter():
    base= SimpleNamespace( address="3420 W GRACE ST",
        city= "CHICAGO", state="IL", zip="60618",
        latitude=41.9503, longitude=-87.7138)
    for row in food_row_iter():
        try:
            parse_details( row )
            row.distance= haversine(
                (row.latitude, row.longitude),
                (base.latitude, base.longitude) )
            yield row
        except TypeError:
            pass
            # print( "problems with", row.dba_name, row.address )
```

This function defines our secret base at 3420 W Grace St. We've already worked out the latitude and longitude, and don't need to make a geocoding request for the location.

For each row produced by `food_row_iter()`, we've used `parse_details()` to update the row. We needed to use a `try:` block because some of the rows have invalid (or missing) latitude and longitude information. When we try to compute `float(None)`, we get a `TypeError` exception. We just skipped those locations. We can geocode them separately, but this is Chicago: there's another restaurant down the block that's probably better.

The result of this function is a sequence of objects that include the distance from our base and health code inspection details. We might, for example, apply some filters to exclude places over .25 miles away or those that got a status of `Fail`:

```
for business in choice_iter():
    if business.distance > .25: continue
    if business.results == "Fail": continue
    print( business.dba_name,
        business.address, business.results,
        len(business.details) )
```

The important thing about this sequence of examples is that we leveraged data from a web source, adding value to the raw data by doing our own intelligence processing. We also combined several individual steps into a more sophisticated composite function.

Final steps

Now that we've located places where we can meet, we have two more things to do. First, we need to create a proper grid code for our chosen locations. The NAC codes are pretty terse. We simply need to agree with our informant about what code we're going to use.

Second, we need to use our steganography script from *Chapter 3, Encoding Secret Messages with Steganography*, to conceal the message in an image. Again, we'll need to be sure that our informant can locate the encoded message in the image.

We'll leave the design of these final processing steps as a mission for you to tackle on your own.

Understanding the data – schema and metadata

Data is described by additional data that we often call metadata. A basic datum might be 6371. Without some metadata, we have no idea what this means. Minimally, metadata has to include the unit of measurement (kilometers in this case) as well the thing being measured (mean radius of the earth).

In the case of less objective data, there may be no units, but rather a domain of possible values. For restaurants, it may be an A-B-C score or a pass-fail outcome. It's important to track down the metadata in order to interpret the actual data.

An additional consideration is the schema problem. A set of data should consist of multiple instances of some essential entity. In our case, the entity is the recent health inspection results for a given restaurant. If each instance has a consistent collection of attributes, we can call that set of attributes the schema for the set of data.

In some cases, the data isn't consistent. Perhaps there are multiple schemata or perhaps the schema is quite complex with options and alternatives. If there's good metadata, it should explain the schema.

The City of Chicago data has a very tidy and complete metadata description for the restaurant health inspection information. We can read it at `https://data.cityofchicago.org/api/assets/BAD5301B-681A-4202-9D25-51B2CAE672FF?download=true`. It explains the risk category assigned to the facility and the ultimate result (pass, pass with conditions, fail). Note the long ugly URL; opaque paths like this are often a bad idea.

The Virginia Department of Health data isn't quite so tidy or complete. We can eventually work out what the data appears to mean. To be completely sure, we'd need to contact the curator of the data to find out precisely what each attribute means. This would involve an e-mail exchange with the department of health at the state level. A field agent might find this extra effort necessary in the case of ambiguous data names.

Summary

In this chapter, we learned how to use web services to perform geocoding and reverse geocoding. We also used web services to get large sets of publicly available information.

We used the `math` library to implement the haversine formula to compute distances between locations. We saw some sophisticated processing, encoding, and decoding techniques and used them to abbreviate grid locations.

We saw more techniques in data gathering using the BeautifulSoup HTML parser. We combined multiple web services to create really sophisticated applications that integrate geocoding and data analysis.

In the next chapter, we'll turn up the sensitivity by performing more sophisticated data analysis using deeper statistical techniques. We'll compute means, modes, and medians and look at correlations among data items.

5
A Spymaster's More Sensitive Analyses

Most of our previous espionage missions focused on bulk data collection and processing. HQ doesn't always want details. Sometimes it needs summaries and assessments. This means calculating central tendencies, summaries, trends, and correlations, which means we need to write more sophisticated algorithms.

We will skirt the borders of some very heavy-duty statistical algorithms. Once we cross the frontier, we will need more powerful tools. For additional tools to support sophisticated numeric processing, check `http://www.numpy.org`. For some analyses, we may be more successful using the SciPy package (`http://www.scipy.org`). A good book to refer is *Learning SciPy for Numerical and Scientific Computing, Francisco J. Blanco-Silva, Packt Publishing* (`http://www.packtpub.com/learning-scipy-for-numerical-and-scientific-computing/book`).

Another direction we could be pulled in includes the analysis of natural language documents. Reports, speeches, books, and articles are sometimes as important as basic facts and figures. If we want to work with words and language, we need to use the **Natural Language Toolkit (NLTK)**. More information on this can be found at `http://www.nltk.org`.

In this chapter, we'll look at several more advanced topics that secret agents need to master, such as:

- Computing *central tendency*—mean, median, and mode—of the data we've gathered.
- Interrogating CSV files to extract information.
- More tips and techniques to use Python generator functions.
- Designing higher-level constructs such as Python modules, libraries, and applications.

- A quick introduction to class definitions.

- Computations of standard deviation, standardized scores, and the coefficient of correlation. This kind of analysis adds value to intelligence assets. Any secret agent can ferret out the raw data. It takes real skill to provide useful summaries.

- How to use doctest to assure that these more sophisticated algorithms really work. Presence of a software bug raises serious questions about the overall quality of the data being reported.

Being a secret agent isn't all car chases and confusing cocktail recipes in posh restaurants. *Shaken? Stirred? Who can remember?*

Sometimes, we need to tackle some rather complex analysis questions that HQ has assigned us. How can we work with per capita cheese consumption, accidental suffocation and strangulation in bed, and the number of doctorates in civil engineering? What Python components should we apply to this problem?

Creating statistical summaries

One essential kind of statistical summary is the *measure of central tendency*. There are several variations on this theme; mean, mode, and median, which are explained as follows:

- The mean, also known as the average, combines all of the values into a single value

- The median is the middlemost value — the data must be sorted to locate the one in the middle

- The mode is the most common value

None of these is perfect to describe a set of data. Data that is truly random can often be summarized by the mean. Data that isn't random, however, can be better summarized by the median. With continuous data, each value might differ slightly from another. Every measurement in a small set of samples may be unique, making a mode meaningless.

As a consequence, we'll need algorithms to compute all three of these essential summaries. First, we need some data to work with.

In *Chapter 2, Acquiring Intelligence Data*, HQ asked us to gather cheese consumption data. We used the URL http://www.ers.usda.gov/datafiles/Dairy_Data/ chezcon_1_.xls.

Sadly, the data was in a format that we can't easily automate, forcing us to copy and paste the annual cheese consumption data. This is what we got. Hopefully, there aren't many errors introduced by copying and pasting. The following is the data that we gathered:

```
year_cheese = [(2000, 29.87), (2001, 30.12), (2002, 30.6), (2003,
30.66),
    (2004, 31.33), (2005, 32.62), (2006, 32.73), (2007, 33.5),
    (2008, 32.84), (2009, 33.02), (2010, 32.92), (2011, 33.27),
    (2012, 33.51)]
```

This will serve as a handy dataset that we can use.

Note that we can type this on multiple lines at the >>> prompt. Python needs to see a matching pair of [and] to consider the statement complete. The matching [] rule allows the users to enter long statements comfortably.

Parsing the raw data file

We've been given the cause of death using ICD code W75 as *accidental suffocation and strangulation in bed*. It's not perfectly clear what HQ thinks this data means. However, it has somehow become important. We went to the http://wonder.cdc.gov website to get the summary of cause of death by year.

We wound up with a file that starts out like this:

```
"Notes"  "Cause of death"  "Cause of death Code"  "Year"  "Year Code"
Deaths  Population  Crude Rate
    "Accidental suffocation and strangulation in bed"  "W75"  "2000"
"2000"  327  281421906  0.1
    "Accidental suffocation and strangulation in bed"  "W75"  "2001"
"2001"  456  284968955  0.2
    … etc. …
```

This is a bit painful to process. It's almost—but not quite—in CSV notation. It's true that there aren't many commas, but there are tab characters encoded as \t in Python. These characters are sufficient to make a CSV file, where the tab takes the role of a comma.

We can read this file using Python's csv module with a \t delimiter:

```
import csv
with open( "Cause of Death by Year.txt" ) as source:
    rdr= csv.DictReader( source, delimiter="\t" )
    for row in rdr:
        if row['Notes'] == "---": break
        print(row)
```

This snippet will create a `csv.DictReader` object using the `\t` delimiter instead of the default value of `,`. Once we have a reader that uses `\t` characters, we can iterate through the rows in the document. Each row will appear as a dictionary. The column title, found in the first row, will be the key for the items in the dictionary.

We used the expression `row['Notes']` to get the value from the `Notes` column of each row. If the notes are equal to `---`, this is the beginning of the footnotes for the data. What follows is a great deal of metadata.

The resulting dataset can be summarized easily. First, we'll create a generator function to parse our data:

```python
def deaths():
    with open( "Cause of Death by Year.txt" ) as source:
        rdr= csv.DictReader( source, delimiter="\t" )
        for row in rdr:
            if row['Notes'] == "Total": break
            yield int(row['Year']), int(row['Deaths'])
```

We replaced the `print()` function with the `yield` statement. We also replaced `---` with `Total` to prune the totals off the data. We can compute our own totals. Finally, we converted the year and deaths to integer values so that we can calculate with them.

This function will iterate through the various rows of data producing two-tuples of the year and the number of deaths.

Once we have this generator function, we can collect the summary like this:

```python
year_deaths = list( deaths() )
```

We get this as a result:

```python
[(2000, 327), (2001, 456), (2002, 509), (2003, 497),
(2004, 596), (2005, 573), (2006, 661), (2007, 741),
(2008, 809), (2009, 717), (2010, 684)]
```

This seems to be the data they're looking for. It gives us more data to work with.

Finding an average value

The mean is defined using a daunting formula which looks like $\mu_x = \frac{\sum_{0 \le i < n} x_i}{n}$. While the formula looks complex, the various parts are first-class built-in functions of Python.

The big sigma $\sum$ is math-speak for the Python `sum()` function.

Given a list of values, the mean is this:

```
def mean( values ):
    return sum(values)/len(values)
```

Our two sets of data are provided as two-tuples with year and amount. We need to reel in the years, stowing away the time for later use. We can use a simple generator function for this. We can use the expression cheese for year, cheese in year_cheese to separate the cheese portion of each two-tuple.

Here's what happens when we use a generator with our mean() function:

```
>>> mean( cheese for year, cheese in year_cheese )
Traceback (most recent call last):
  File "<stdin>", line 1, in <module>
  File "<stdin>", line 2, in mean
TypeError: object of type 'generator' has no len()
```

Wait. What?

How can the simple generator not work?

Actually, it does work. It just doesn't do what we assume.

Understanding generator expressions

There are three important rules that apply to Python generators:

- Many—but not all—functions will work with generator objects. Some functions, however, will not work well with generators; they require a sequence object.

- The objects yielded by a generator aren't created until absolutely necessary. We can describe a generator as being lazy. A list, for example, actually contains objects. A generator expression can operate similarly to a list, but the objects aren't really created until needed.

- Generator functions can only be used once. A list can be reused indefinitely.

The first restriction applies in particular to the len() function. This function works for lists, tuples, and sets. However, it doesn't work for generators. There's no way to know how many items will eventually be created by a generator, so len() can't return the size.

The second restriction is mostly relevant when we try to print the results of a generator. We'll see something such as <generator object <genexpr> at 0x1007b4460>, until we actually evaluate the generator and create the objects.

The third restriction is less obvious. We will to need an example. Let's try to work around the len() problem by defining a count() function that counts items yielded by a generator function:

```
def count( values ):
    return sum( 1 for x in values )
```

This will add up a sequence of 1s instead of the sequence of actual values.

We can test it like this:

```
>>> count( cheese for year, cheese in year_cheese )
13
```

This seems to work, right? Based on this one experiment, we can try to rewrite the mean() function like this:

```
def mean2( values ):
    return sum(values)/count(values)
```

We used count(), which works with a generator expression, instead of len().

When we use it, we get a ZeroDivisionError: float division by zero error. Why didn't count() work in the context of mean()?

This reveals the one-use-only rule. The sum() function consumed the generator expression. When the time to evaluate the count() function came, there was no data left. The generator was empty, sum(1 for x in []) was zero.

What can we do?

We have three choices, as follows:

- We can write our own more sophisticated sum() that produces both sum and count from one pass through the generator.
- Alternatively, we can use the itertools library to put a *tee* fitting into the generator pipeline so that we have two copies of the iterable. This is actually a very efficient solution, but it's also a bit advanced for field agents.
- More simply, we can create an actual list object from the generator. We can use the list() function or wrap the generator expression in [].

The first two choices are too complex for our purposes. The third is really simple. We can use this:

```
>>> mean( [cheese for year, cheese in year_cheese] )
32.076153846153844
>>> mean( [death for year, death in year_deaths] )
597.2727272727273
```

By including `[]`, we created a list object from the generator. We can get both `sum()` and `len()` from the list object. This approach works very nicely.

It points out the importance of writing docstrings in our functions. We really need to do this:

```
def mean(values):
    """Mean of a sequence (doesn't work with an iterable)"""
    return sum(values)/len(values)
```

We put a reminder here that the function works with an object that is a sequence, but it doesn't work with a generator expression or other objects that are merely iterable. When we use `help(mean)`, we'll see the reminder we left in the docstring.

There's a hierarchy of concepts here. Being iterable is a very general feature of many kinds of Python objects. A sequence is one of many kinds of iterable Python objects.

Finding the value in the middle

The median value is in the middle of a sorted collection of values. In order to find the median, we need to sort the data.

Here's an easy function to compute the median of a sequence:

```
def median(values):
    s = sorted(values)
    if len(s) % 2 == 1: # Odd
        return s[len(s)//2]
    else:
        mid= len(s)//2
        return (s[mid-1]+s[mid])/2
```

This includes the common technique of averaging the two middlemost values when there's an even number of samples.

We used `len(s)%2` to determine if the sequence length is odd. In two separate places, we compute `len(s)//2`; seems like we might be able to simplify things using the `divmod()` function.

We can use this:

```
mid, odd = divmod(len(s), 2)
```

This change removes a little bit of the duplicated code that computes `len(s)//2`, but is it really more clear?

Two potential issues here are the overheads associated with sorting:

- First, sorting means a lot of comparisons between items. As the size of the list grows, the number of items compared grows more quickly. Also, the `sorted()` function produces a copy of the sequence, potentially wasting memory when processing a very large list.
- The alternative is a clever variation on the quickselect algorithm. For field agents, this level of sophistication isn't necessary. More information is available at `http://en.wikipedia.org/wiki/Quickselect`.

Finding the most popular value

The modal value is the single most popular value in the collection. We can compute this using the `Counter` class in the `collections` module.

Here's a `mode` function:

```
from collections import Counter
def mode(values):
    c = Counter( values )
    mode_value, count = c.most_common(1)[0]
    return mode_value
```

The `most_common()` method of a `Counter` class returns a sequence of two-tuples. Each tuple has the value and the number of times it occurred. For our purposes, we only wanted the value, so we had to take the first element from the sequence of two-tuples. Then, we had to break the pair down into the value and the counter.

The problem with a demonstration is that our datasets are really small and don't have a proper mode. Here's a contrived example:

```
>>> mode( [1, 2, 3, 3, 4] )
3
```

This demonstrates that the `mode` function works, even though it doesn't make sense for our cheese consumption and death rate data.

Creating Python modules and applications

We relied heavily on modules in the Python library. Additionally, we added several packages, including Pillow and BeautifulSoup. The question should arise, *can we create our own module?*

The answer is, of course, *yes*. A Python module is simply a file. It turns out that each example script has been a module. We can look a little more deeply at how we can make our own modules of reusable programming. When we look at Python programs, we observe three kinds of files:

- Library modules that are purely definitional
- Application modules that do the real work of our applications
- Hybrid modules that are both applications and can be used as libraries

The essential ingredient of creating a Python module is separating the *real work* of the top-level script from the various definitions that support this real work. All our examples of definitions have been functions created with the def statement. The other import examples of definitions are class definitions, which we'll discuss in the following sections.

Creating and using a module

To create a module of only definitions, we simply put all the function and class definitions into a file. We have to give the file a name that is an acceptable Python variable name. This means that filenames should look like Python variables; letters, digits, and _ are perfectly legal. Characters that Python uses as an operator (+, -, /, and so on) may be allowed by our OS for a filename, but these characters cannot be used to name a module file.

The file name must end in .py. This is not part of the module name; it's for the benefit of the operating system.

We might collect our statistics functions into a file named stats.py. This file defines a module named stats.

We can import the entire suite of functions or individual functions, or we can import the module as a whole. Use the following code:

```
>>> from stats import *
```

By using this, we import all the functions (and classes) defined in the stats module. We can simply use names such as mean(some_list).

Consider we use this:

```
>>> from stats import mean, median
```

We imported two specific functions from the stats module. We ignored any other definition that might be available in that module.

We can also use this:

```
>>> import stats
```

This will import the module, but it won't put any of the names into the global namespace that we usually work with. All the names in the `stats` module must be accessed with a qualified name, such as `stats.mean( some_list )`. In very complex scripts, the use of qualified names helps clarify where a particular function or class was defined.

Creating an application module

The simplest way to create an application with a **command-line interface (CLI)** is to write a file and run it from the command line. Consider the following example:

```
python3 basic_stats.py
```

When we enter this in the terminal window or command window, we use the OS `python3` command and provide a filename. In Windows, the name `python.exe` is sometimes used for Python 3, so the command may be `python basic_stats.py`. In most other OSes, there will often be both the `python3` and `python3.3` commands. On Mac OS X, the `python` command may refer to the old `Python2.7` that is part of Mac OS X.

We can determine the difference by using the `python -V` command to see what version is bound to the name `python`.

As noted previously, we want to separate our definitions into one file, and then put the real work in another file. When we look inside `basic_stats.py`, we might find this:

```
"""Chapter 5 example 2.

Import stats library functions from ch_5_ex_1 module.
Import data acquisition from ch_5_ex_1 module.
Compute some simple descriptive statistics.
"""
from ch_5_ex_1 import mean, mode, median
from ch_5_ex_1 import get_deaths, get_cheese

year_deaths = list( get_deaths() )
years = list( year for year, death in year_deaths )
deaths= list( death for year, death in year_deaths )
print( "Year Range", min(years), "to", max(years) )
print( "Average Deaths {:.2f}".format( mean( deaths ) ) )
```

```
year_cheese= get_cheese()

print( "Average Cheese Consumption",
    mean( [cheese for year, cheese in year_cheese] ) )
```

The file starts with a triple-quoted string that—like the docstring for a function—is the docstring for a module. We imported some functions from another module.

Then, we completed some processing using the functions that we imported. This is a common structure for a simple command-line module.

We can also run this via the command python3 -m basic_stats. This will use Python's internal search path to locate the module, and then run that module. Running a module is subtly different from running a file, but the net effect is the same; the file produces the output we designed via the print() statements. For details on how the -m option works, consult the documentation for the runpy module.

Creating a hybrid module

There are two significant improvements we can make to the basic_stats.py module shown previously:

- First, we put all the processing into a function definition. We call it analyze_cheese_deaths.

- The second is the addition of an if statement to determine the context in which the module is being used.

Here's the more sophisticated version of basic_stats.py:

```
"""Chapter 5 example 3.

Import stats library functions from ch_5_ex_1 module.
Import data acquisition from ch_5_ex_1 module.
Compute some simple descriptive statistics.
"""
from ch_5_ex_1 import mean, mode, median
from ch_5_ex_1 import get_deaths, get_cheese

def analyze_cheese_deaths():

    year_deaths = list( get_deaths() )
    years = list( year for year, death in year_deaths )
    deaths= list( death for year, death in year_deaths )
    print( "Year Range", min(years), "to", max(years) )
    print( "Average Deaths {:.2f}".format( mean( deaths ) ) )
```

```
        year_cheese= get_cheese()
        print( "Average Cheese Consumption",
            mean( [cheese for year, cheese in year_cheese] ) )

    if __name__ == "__main__":
        analyze_cheese_deaths()
```

Creating a function definition to encapsulate the real work gives us a way to extend or reuse this script. We can reuse a function definition (via `import`) more easily than we can reuse a top-level script.

The `__name__` variable is a global that Python sets to show the processing context. The top-level module—the one named on the command line—has the `__name__` variable set to `__main__`. All other module imports have the `__name__` variable set to the module name.

Yes, the global variable, `__name__`, has double-underscores before and after. This marks it as part of the machinery of Python. Similarly, the string value for the main module name, `__main__`, involves double underscores.

This technique allows us to create a module that can be run as a command and also be imported to provide definitions. The idea is to promote reusable programming. Each time we set out to solve a problem, we don't need to reinvent the wheel and other related technology. We should import prior work and build on that.

Creating our own classes of objects

The two lists of data values that HQ asked us to get—cheese consumption and W75 deaths—form two objects that are very similar. They seem to be two instances of the same class of things.

In this case, the class of things seems to have *annual statistics*. They're collections with a consistent structure of a year and a measurement. Both these annual statistics objects have a common set of operations. Indeed, the operations are pretty tightly bound to the measurement, and they are not at all bound to the year number.

Our collection of statistical functions is not very tightly bound to our data at all.

We can improve the binding between data structure and processing through a class definition. If we define the general features of a class of objects that we can call *annual statistics*, we can create two instances of this class and use the defined methods on the unique data of each instance. We can easily reuse our method functions by having multiple objects of the same class.

A class definition in Python is a collection of method functions. Each method function definition has an additional parameter variable, usually named `self`, which must be the first parameter to each function. The self variable is how we can access the attribute values that are unique to each instance of the class of objects.

Here's how we might define a class for the simple statistics HQ is asking us to get:

```
from collections import Counter
class AnnualStats:
    def __init__(self, year_measure):
        self.year_measure = list(year_measure)
        self.data = list(v for yr, v in self.year_measure)
        self.counter= Counter(self.data)
    def __repr__(self):
        return repr(self.year_measure)
    def min_year(self):
        return min( yr for yr, v in self.year_measure )
    def max_year(self):
        return max( yr for yr, v in self.year_measure )
    def mean(self):
        return sum(self.data)/len(self.data)
    def median(self):
        mid, odd = divmod( len(self.data), 2 )
        if odd:
            return sorted(self.data)[mid]
        else:
            pair= sorted(self.data)[mid-1:mid+1]
            return sum(pair)/2
    def mode(self):
        value, count = self.counter.most_common1)[0]
        return value
```

The `class` statement provides a name for our definition. Within the indented body of the class statement, we provide `def` statements for each method function within this class. Each `def` statement contains the instance variable, `self`.

We've defined two methods with special names, as shown in the following list. These names have double underscores, they're fixed by Python, and we must use exactly these names in order to have objects initialized or printed properly:

- The `__init__()` method is used implicitly to initialize the instance when it's created. We'll show an example of instance creation in the following section. When we create an `AnnualStats` object, three internal attributes are created, as shown in the following list:

    ○ The `self.year_measure` instance variable contains the data provided as an argument value

- The `self.data` instance variable contains just the data values extracted from the year-data two-tuples
- The `self.counter` instance variable contains a `Counter` object built from the data values

- The `__repr__()` method is used implicitly when we attempt to print the object. We returned the representation of the internal `self.year_measure` instance variable as the representation for the instance as a whole.

The other method functions look similar to the standalone function definitions shown previously. Each of these method functions depend on having the instance variables properly initialized by the `__init__()` method. These names are entirely part of our software design; we can call them anything that's syntactically legal and meaningful.

Using a class definition

Here's how we can use our `AnnualStats` class definition:

```
from ch_5_ex_1 import get_deaths, get_cheese

deaths = AnnualStats( get_deaths() )
cheese = AnnualStats( get_cheese() )

print("Year Range", deaths.min_year(), deaths.max_year())
print("Average W75 Deaths", deaths.mean())

print("Median Cheese Consumption", cheese.median())
print("Mean Cheese Consumption", cheese.mean())

print(deaths )
```

We built two instances of the `AnnualStats` class. The `deaths` object is an `AnnualStats` object built from the year-death set of data. Similarly, the `cheese` object is an `AnnualStats` object built from the cheese consumption set of data.

In both cases, the `AnnualStats.__init__()` method is evaluated with the given argument value. When we evaluate `AnnualStats( get_deaths() )`, the result of `get_deaths()` is provided to `AnnualStats.__init__()` as the value of the `year_measure` parameter. The statements of the `__init__()` method will then set the values of the three instance variables.

When we evaluate `deaths.min_year()`, this will evaluate the `AnnualStats.min_year()` method function. The `self` variable will be `deaths`. This means that `self.year_measure` denotes the object originally created by `get_deaths()`.

When we evaluate `deaths.mean()`, this will evaluate the `AnnualStats.min_year()` method function with the `self` variable referring to deaths. This means `deaths.data` is the sorted sequence we derived from the object originally created by `get_deaths()`.

Each instance (`deaths`, `cheese`) refers to the instance variables created by the `__init__()` method. A class encapsulates the processing of the method functions with the various instance variables. The encapsulation idea can help us design software that is more tightly focused and less likely to have confusing bugs or inconsistencies.

Comparisons and correlations

An important statistical question centers around correlation between variables. We often wonder if two sequences of values correlate with each other. If we have variables that correlate, perhaps we've found an interesting causal relationship. We might be able to use one variable to predict the values of another variable. We might also be able to prove that they're independent and have nothing to do with each other.

The essential statistical tool for this is the *coefficient of correlation*. We have several ways to compute this. One solution is to download NumPy or SciPy from the following links:

- `http://docs.scipy.org/doc/scipy/reference/generated/scipy.stats.pearsonr.html`
- `http://docs.scipy.org/doc/numpy/reference/generated/numpy.corrcoef.html`

The correlation algorithms, however, aren't too complex. Implementing these two calculations will build up our basic data gathering espionage skills. We'll build some more basic statistical functions. Then, we'll build the correlation calculation, which will depend on other statistical functions.

The essential numerical depends on computing means and standard deviations. We looked at the mean calculation previously. We'll add the standard deviation to our bag of tricks. Given the standard deviation, we can standardize each value. We'll compute the distance from the mean using the standard deviation as the measurement of distance. We can then compare standardized scores to see if two sets of data correlate.

Computing the standard deviation

To compute the correlation coefficient, we need another descriptive statistic for a set of data: the standard deviation. This is a measure of how widely dispersed the data is. When we compute the mean, we find a center for the data. The next question is, *how tightly do the values huddle around the center?*

If the standard deviation is small, the data is tightly clustered. If the standard deviation is large, the data is spread all over the place. The standard deviation calculation gives us a numeric range that brackets about two-third of the data values.

Having the standard deviation lets us spot unusual data. For example, the mean cheese consumption is 31.8 pounds per person. The standard deviation is 1.27 pounds. We expect to see much of the data huddled within the range of 31.8 ± 1.27, that is, between 30.53 and 33.07. If our informant tries to tell as the per capita cheese consumption is 36 pounds in 2012, we have a good reason to be suspicious of the report.

There are a few variations to the theme of computing a standard deviation. There are some statistical subtleties, also, that relate to whether or not we have the entire population or just a sample. Here's one of the standard formulae $\sigma_x = \sqrt{\frac{1}{n} \Sigma (x_i - \mu_x)^2}$. The symbol σ_x represents the standard deviation of some variable, x. The symbol μ_x represents the mean of a variable.

We have a method function, `mean()`, which computes the μ_x value. We need to implement the standard deviation formula.

The standard deviation formula uses the `math.sqrt()` and `sum()` functions. We'll rely on using `import math` in our script.

We can directly translate the equation into Python. Here's a method function we can add to our `AnnualStat` class:

```python
def stddev(self):
    µ_x = self.mean()
    n = len(self.data)
    σ_x= math.sqrt( sum( (x-µ_x)**2 for x in self.data )/n )
    return σ_x
```

We evaluated the `mean()` method function to get the mean, shown as μ_x, and assigned this to µ_x (yes, Greek letters are legal for Python variable names; if your OS doesn't offer ready access to extended Unicode characters, you might want to use `mu` instead). We also evaluated `len(data)` to get the value of n, the number of elements in the collection.

We can then do a very literal translation from math-speak to Python. For example, the $\Sigma(x-\mu_x)^2$ becomes `sum((x-μ_x)**2 for x in self.data)`. This kind of literal match between mathematical notation and Python makes it easy to vet Python programming to be sure it matches the mathematical abstraction.

Here's another version of standard deviation, based on a slightly different formula:

```
def stddev2(self):
    s_0 = sum(1 for x in self.data) # x**0
    s_1 = sum(x for x in self.data) # x**1
    s_2 = sum(x**2 for x in self.data)
    return math.sqrt( s_2/s_0 - (s_1/s_0)**2 )
```

This has an elegant symmetry to it. The formula looks like $\sigma_x = \sqrt{\dfrac{\sum x^2}{n} - \left(\dfrac{\sum x}{n}\right)^2}$.
It's not efficient or accurate any more. It's just sort of cool because of the symmetry between $\sum x^0 = n$, $\sum x^1$, and $\sum x^2$.

Computing a standardized score

Once we have the standard deviation, we can standardize each measurement in the sequence. This standardized score is sometimes called a Z score. It's the number of standard deviations a particular value lies from the mean.

In $S(x_i) = \dfrac{(x_i - \mu_x)}{\sigma_x}$, the standardized score, $S(x_i)$, is the difference between the score, x_i, and the mean, μ_x, divided by the standard deviation, σ_x.

If we have a mean, μ, of 31.8 and a standard deviation, σ, of 1.27, then a measured value of 29.87 will have a Z score of -1.519. About 30 percent of the data will be outside 1 standard deviation from the mean. When our informant tries to tell us that consumption jumped to 36 pounds of cheese per capita, we can compute the Z score for this, 3.307, and suggest that it's unlikely to be valid data.

Standardizing our values to produce scores is a great use of a generator expression. We'll add this to our class definition too:

```
def stdscore(self):
    μ_x= self.mean()
    σ_x= self.stddev()
    return [ (x-μ_x)/σ_x for x in self.data ]
```

We computed the mean of our data and assigned it to μ_x. We computed the standard deviation and assigned it to σ_x. We used a generator expression to evaluate `(x-μ_x)/σ_x` for each value, x, in our data. Since the generator was in [], we will create a new list object with the standardized scores.

We can show how this works with this:

```
print( cheese.stdscore() )
```

We'll get a sequence like the following:

```
[-1.548932453971435, -1.3520949193863403, ... 0.8524854679667219]
```

Comparing a sequence and an iterable

When we look at the result of the `stdscore()` method, we have a choice of what to return. In the previous example, we returned a new list object. We don't really need to do this.

We can use this in the function to return a generator instead of a list:

```
return ((x-μ_x)/σ_x for x in self.data)
```

The rest of the function is the same. It's good to give this version a different name. Call the old one `stdscore2()` so that you can compare list and generator versions.

The generator `stdscore()` function now returns an expression that can be used to generate the values. For most of our calculations, there's no practical difference between an actual list object and an iterable sequence of values.

There are three differences that we'll notice:

- Firstly, we can't use `len()` on the generator results
- Secondly, a generator doesn't generate any data until we use it in a `for` loop or to create a list
- Thirdly, an iterable can only be used once

Try to see how this works with something simple like this:

```
print(cheese.stdscore())
```

We'll see the generator expression, not the values that are generated. Here's the output:

```
<generator object <genexpr> at 0x1007b4460>
```

We need to do this to collect the generated values into an object. The `list()` function does this nicely. Here's what we can do to evaluate the generator and actually generate the values:

```
print(list(cheese.stdscore()))
```

This will evaluate the generator, producing a list object that we can print.

Computing a coefficient of correlation

One important question that arises when comparing two sequences of data is how well they correlate with each other. When one sequence trends up, does the other? Do they trend at the same rate? We can measure this correlation by computing a coefficient based on the products of the standardized scores:

$$r = \frac{1}{n}\sum s\left(x_i\right) \times s\left(y_i\right)$$

In this case, $s\left(x_i\right)$ is the standardized score for each individual value, $s(x_i) = \frac{(x_i - \mu_x)}{\sigma_x}$. We do the same calculation for the other sequences and compute the product of each pair. The average of the product of the various standardized scores will be a value between +1 and -1. A value near +1 means the two sequences correlate nicely. A value near -1 means the sequences oppose each other. One trends up when the other trends down. A value near 0 means the sequences don't correlate.

Here's a function that computes the correlation between two instances of `AnnualStat` data collections:

```
def correlation1( d1, d2 ):
    n= len(d1.data)
    std_score_pairs = zip( d1.stdscore(), d2.stdscore() )
    r = sum( x*y for x,y in std_score_pairs )/n
    return r
```

We used the `stdscore()` method of each `AnnualStat` object to create a sequence of standardized score values.

We created a generator using the `zip()` function that will yield two-tuples from two separate sequences of scores. The mean of this sequence of products is the coefficient correlation between the two sequences. We computed the mean by summing and dividing by the length, n.

Writing high-quality software

How do we know these various statistical functions work? This is potentially very tricky programming, with lots of opportunities to have things go wrong.

The best tool to make sure that software works is unit testing. The idea behind unit testing is to break a module down into separate units—usually functions or classes—and test each unit in isolation. Python gives us two ways to perform unit testing:

- Putting examples into docstrings for modules, functions, and classes
- Writing separate `unittest.TestCase` classes

Most secret agents will be very happy with docstring test cases. They're easy to write. We put them in the docstring right in front of the rest of the code. They're visible when we use the `help()` function.

We create these docstring test cases by copying and pasting known correct results from interactive Python. The copy and paste will include the `>>>` prompt to make it easy to find the examples. Of course, we also include the output that's expected. Once we include this in the docstring, the `doctest` module will find and use the example.

In some cases, we need to fake the expected results. It's actually common to have worked out what the answer is supposed to be before having written any working Python code. If we're sure the docstring example has the expected right answer, we can leverage this and use it to help debug the code.

Let's look at a simple function we wrote earlier:

```python
def mean(values):
    """Mean of a sequence (doesn't work with an iterable)

    >>> from ch_5_ex_1 import mean
    >>> mean( [2, 4, 4, 4, 5, 5, 7, 9])
    5.0
    """
    return sum(values)/len(values)
```

We added the example interaction to the function's docstring. We included what looks like a copy and paste of the sequence of interactions that will exercise this function. In some cases, we make the sequence up based on what we plan to write, not what we've written.

We can exercise the several different ways. The easiest is this:

```
python3 -m doctest ch_5_ex_1.py
```

We run the `doctest` module as a top-level main application. The single argument to this application is the name of a Python application that has doctest examples pasted into docstrings.

There's no output if everything works. If we're curious, we can ask for more verbose output:

```
python3 -m doctest -v ch_5_ex_1.py
```

This will produce voluminous output that shows each test that was found in the docstrings in the module.

The other techniques include building a self-testing module and writing a separate script that just runs tests.

Building a self-testing module and a test module

One of the techniques that works out nicely is using the `__name__ == "__main__"` technique to add a test script to a library module. We'll evaluate the `doctest.testmod()` function to test the functions and classes defined in a module.

It looks like this:

```
if __name__ == "__main__":
    import doctest
    doctest.testmod()
```

If this module is being run from the command line, it's the main module, and global `__name__` will be set to `"__main__"`. When this is true, we can import the doctest module and evaluate `doctest.testmod()` to confirm that everything else in the module works.

We can also write a separate test script. We might call it `"test.py"`; it might be as short as this:

```
import doctest
import ch_5_ex_1
doctest.testmod( ch_5_ex_1 )
```

This short script imported the doctest module. It also imported the module we're going to test.

We used the `doctest.testmod()` function to locate doctest examples in the given module. The output looks like this:

```
TestResults(failed=0, attempted=2)
```

This is a confirmation that there were two lines of `>>>` examples, and everything worked perfectly.

Creating more sophisticated tests

There are times when we have to be a little cautious of the doctest example output. These are situations where Python's behavior is not specified to the level of detail where we can copy and paste interactive results without thinking about what we're doing.

When working with dict and set collections, the order of the items is not guaranteed.

- For a dict, a doctest string needs to include `sorted()` to force a specific order. It's essential to use `sorted(some_dict.items())` instead of simply using `some_dict`.

- The same consideration applies to sets. We must use something like `sorted(some_set)` instead of `some_set`.

Some internal functions such as `id()` and `repr()` can display a physical memory address that's unlikely to be the same each time we run the tests. There's a special comment we can include that will alert doctest to skip the details. We'll include `#doctest: +ELLIPSIS` and replace the ID or address with . . . (three dots).

Another place we might use ellipsis is to shorten up a very long bit of output.

For example, we might have a module docstring like this:

```
"""Chapter 5, example 1

Some simple statistical functions.

>>> from ch_5_ex_1 import mean, median
>>> data = [2, 4, 4, 4, 5, 5, 7, 9]
>>> data # doctest: +ELLIPSIS
[2, 4..., 9]
>>> mean( data )
5.0
>>> median( data )
4.5

"""
```

A module docstring must be (almost) the first lines in a module file. The only line that might come before the module docstring is a one-line `#!` comment. A `#!` comment line, if present, is aimed at the OS shell and identifies the rest of the file as being a Python script, not a shell script.

We used the # doctest: +ELLIPSIS directive on one of our tests. The result wasn't complete, it had "..." in the expected results to show the parts doctest should ignore.

Floating-point values may not be identical for different processors and OSes. We have to be careful to show floating-point numbers with formatting or rounding. We might use "{:.4f}".format(value) or round(value,4) to assure that the insignificant digits are ignored.

Adding doctest cases to a class definition

We looked at doctests in modules and functions. We can put doctests in several places in a class definition. This is because we have several places to put docstrings.

The class as a whole can have a docstring right at the top. It's the first line after the class statement. Also, each individual method within a class can have its own private docstring.

We might, for example, include a comprehensive docstring at the beginning of our class definition:

```
class AnnualStats:
    """Collect (year, measurement) data for statistical analysis.

    >>> from ch_5_ex_4 import AnnualStats
    >>> test = AnnualStats( [(2000, 2),
    ...     (2001, 4),
    ...     (2002, 4),
    ...     (2003, 4),
    ...     (2004, 5),
    ...     (2005, 5),
    ...     (2006, 7),
    ...     (2007, 9),] )
    ...
    >>> test.min_year()
    2000
    >>> test.max_year()
    2007
    >>> test.mean()
    5.0
    >>> test.median()
    4.5
    >>> test.mode()
    4
    >>> test.stddev()
    2.0
    >>> list(test.stdscore())
    [-1.5, -0.5, -0.5, -0.5, 0.0, 0.0, 1.0, 2.0]
    """
```

This provides a complete rundown of all of the features of this class in one tidy summary.

[Our sample data leads to a standard deviation of exactly 2.0. This trick shows that with clever test data, we can circumvent some of the doctest float-point output limitations.]

Solving problems – analyzing some interesting datasets

What is the correlation coefficient between per-capita cheese consumption and death code W75 (accidental suffocation and strangulation in bed) for the years 2000 to 2009?

Recall that the cheese data came from `http://www.ers.usda.gov/datafiles/ Dairy_Data/chezcon_1_.xls`.

This is a pesky bit of data because it's in a proprietary spreadsheet format. As much as we dislike copying and pasting, there's no other easy way to get this data.

The strangulation in bed data comes from cause of death W75 grouped by year. The data request process starts at `http://wonder.cdc.gov/controller/datarequest/ D76`. There will be some further espionage work required to enter a request for data. For some additional help, check `http://wonder.cdc.gov/wonder/help/ucd.html`.

How the correlation possibly be so high?

What is it about cheese consumption and death by strangulation in bed that leads to this amazing correlation?

Getting some more data

HQ appears to be working on a theory about dairy products. The cheese spreadsheet also has mozzarella cheese consumption over the same period of time—2000 to 2009.

We've been ordered to get details on civil engineering doctorates awarded during this period.

Some initial espionage turned up this set of data:

`http://www.nsf.gov/statistics/infbrief/nsf12303/`

This is a tricky table to parse. It's a bit more complex because the years are in columns and the data we're looking for is in a particular row, a row with `th.text == "Civil engineering"`. The heading for the table as a whole is in a row with `th.text == "Field"`. This means that the navigation will be rather complex to locate the `Field` row and the `Civil engineering` rows of the proper table on this page.

How does annual per-capita mozzarella cheese consumption correlate with civil engineering doctorates?

How can the correlation possibly be so high?

What is it about cheese, death, and doctorates?

Further research

Is this just a spurious correlation?

Are there other correlations like this?

What else can we learn from `http://www.tylervigen.com/`?

Summary

We saw how we can easily implement sophisticated statistical analyses as short pieces of Python programming. We applied basic statistical insights to all our intelligence gathering.

We learned to design Python modules. This allows us to extend the Python standard library with our own more specialized modules. We can now easily package reusable software in modules for our own purposes as well as for distribution to our network of agents.

In addition to designing modules, we also saw how to write tests to confirm that our software really works. Software can't be trusted unless there are formal unit tests to confirm that things are behaving correctly. We saw the essential ingredients of the Python language, the standard library, and the ecosystem of related projects and tools. The Python language is quite simple: it only has about 22 statements, and we saw examples of almost all of them.

At this point, each secret agent's areas of interest and expertise will start to diverge. There are numerous packages, libraries, and application areas that are open for exploration.

Since our focus is on getting field agents to be productive, we were studiously avoiding more serious software development issues. In particular, we avoided the subject of object-oriented design. An agent that needs to do more sophisticated processing will need to write more sophisticated software. A book like *Python 3 Object Oriented Programming, Dusty Phillips, Packt Publishing*, is essential to learn this important technique. Check `http://www.packtpub.com/python-3-object-oriented-programming/book`.

An agent's interests and abilities will often lead in different directions. Some agents will want to build websites. A book like *Python 3 Web Development Beginner's Guide, Michel Anders, Packt Publishing*, can help. Some agents will want to build interactive applications; a book like *Instant Pygame for Python Game Development How-to, Ivan Idris, Packt Publishing*, can help master the Pygame framework. This framework is for more than just games.

Some agents will pursue natural language processing. A book like *Python 3 Text Processing with NLTK 3 Cookbook, Jacob Perkins, Packt Publishing*, can help. Other agents will pursue more complex media using *Python Multimedia, Ninad Sathaye, Packt Publishing* or perhaps *Practical Maya Programming with Python, Robert Galanakis, Packt Publishing*. Agents interested in geospatial analysis might pursue *Programming ArcGIS 10.1 with Python Cookbook, Eric Pimpler, Packt Publishing*.

Skilled agents will find that Python can be used for a wide variety of missions.

Index

Symbols

A

B

C

N

NAC (Natural Area Code)
about 143
creating 143-145
decoding 146
namespace 149
Natural Language Toolkit (NLTK)
URL 38, 165
neighborhoods 123
numbers
about 14
values, assigning to variables 21, 22
NumPy
URL 165

O

open() function 33
OS filesystem
glob module 80, 81
os package 81
os package, OS filesystem 81

P

parse_details() method 162
partition() method 35
Pillow
about 79
confirming 89, 90
documentation, URL 87
image data, decoding 91-93
image data, encoding 91-93
images, cropping 95-98
images, filtering 100, 101
images, resizing 94
installing 89, 90
slice details, enhancing 99
supporting libraries, adding 87
URL 87
PIP
URL 11
pixels 86
prime meridian 122
print() function 24, 31, 33
projection 122

PyCrypto package
URL 116
pySerial project
URL 123
Python
about 8
exit() option 12
FTP, using 49
help mode, using 14
help() system, using 12, 13
REST API, using 55
testing 11, 12
URL, for download 8
Python 3.3
about 8
Mac OS X installer 9
Windows installer 8
Python applications, creating
developer tools, obtaining 10
text editor, using 9, 10
Python dictionary mapping
access methods, using 67, 68
using 66, 67
Python generators
rules 169
Python Imaging Library (PIL) 87
Python list
list index operations, using 61, 62
using 60, 61
Python module
about 173
application module, creating 174, 175
creating 173
hybrid module, creating 175, 176
using 173
Python modules, adding
easy_install, using 10
PIP, using 11
Python object
creating 148, 149
creating, from columns of data 154
creating, from JSON document 160-162
enriching, with geocodes 155
enriching, with health scores 156, 157
Python operators
difference (-) 74
intersection (&) 74

T

table
  parsing 152, 153
tags 86
tampering
  detecting 115
  hash totals, using 115
  key, adding to message digest 116
  preventing 115
test module
  building 185
text
  handling 27, 28
text editor
  using 9, 10
text files
  processing 81, 82
thumbnail
  creating 94, 95
tools, HTML web services
  Easy Install 150
  scrapy 150

U

Unicode characters
  bytes, extracting 105, 106
unit testing
  about 184
  performing 184
urllib
  using, for file access 54
  using, for FTP access 54
  using, for HTTP 53
urllib.parse.urlencode() function 57
user agent string
  URL 48

user input
  exceptions, handling 25, 26
  gathering 24, 25
  looping 26, 27
User Interface (UI) 23

V

values
  assigning, to variables 21, 22

W

Windows
  Pillow distribution libraries 89
Windows installer, Python3.3 9
word corpus, lost password recovery
  reading 38, 39
World Wide Web (WWW) 43

X

Xcode
  URL 10, 88

Y

Yelp
  URL 147

Z

ZIP archive, lost password recovery
  reading 39, 40
ZIP files
  working with 83

Thank you for buying
Python for Secret Agents

About Packt Publishing

Packt, pronounced 'packed', published its first book "*Mastering phpMyAdmin for Effective MySQL Management*" in April 2004 and subsequently continued to specialize in publishing highly focused books on specific technologies and solutions.

Our books and publications share the experiences of your fellow IT professionals in adapting and customizing today's systems, applications, and frameworks. Our solution based books give you the knowledge and power to customize the software and technologies you're using to get the job done. Packt books are more specific and less general than the IT books you have seen in the past. Our unique business model allows us to bring you more focused information, giving you more of what you need to know, and less of what you don't.

Packt is a modern, yet unique publishing company, which focuses on producing quality, cutting-edge books for communities of developers, administrators, and newbies alike. For more information, please visit our website: www.packtpub.com.

About Packt Open Source

In 2010, Packt launched two new brands, Packt Open Source and Packt Enterprise, in order to continue its focus on specialization. This book is part of the Packt Open Source brand, home to books published on software built around Open Source licenses, and offering information to anybody from advanced developers to budding web designers. The Open Source brand also runs Packt's Open Source Royalty Scheme, by which Packt gives a royalty to each Open Source project about whose software a book is sold.

Writing for Packt

We welcome all inquiries from people who are interested in authoring. Book proposals should be sent to author@packtpub.com. If your book idea is still at an early stage and you would like to discuss it first before writing a formal book proposal, contact us; one of our commissioning editors will get in touch with you.

We're not just looking for published authors; if you have strong technical skills but no writing experience, our experienced editors can help you develop a writing career, or simply get some additional reward for your expertise.

Raspberry Pi for Secret Agents

ISBN: 978-1-84969-578-7 Paperback: 152 pages

Turn your Raspberry Pi into your very own secret agent toolbox with this set of exciting projects!

1. Detect an intruder on camera and set off an alarm.

2. Listen in or record conversations from a distance.

3. Find out what the other computers on your network are up to.

4. Unleash your Raspberry Pi on the world.

Raspberry Pi Robotic Projects

ISBN: 978-1-84969-432-2 Paperback: 278 pages

Create amazing robotic projects on a shoestring budget

1. Make your projects talk and understand speech with Raspberry Pi.

2. Use standard webcam to make your projects see and enhance vision capabilities.

3. Full of simple, easy-to-understand instructions to bring your Raspberry Pi online for developing robotics projects.

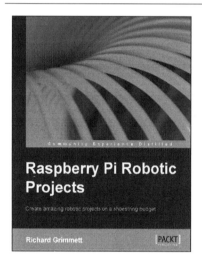

Please check **www.PacktPub.com** for information on our titles

Python High Performance Programming

ISBN: 978-1-78328-845-8   Paperback: 108 pages

Boost the performance of your Python programs using advanced techniques

1. Identify the bottlenecks in your applications and solve them using the best profiling techniques.

2. Write efficient numerical code in NumPy and Cython.

3. Adapt your programs to run on multiple processors with parallel programming.

OpenCV Computer Vision with Python

ISBN: 978-1-78216-392-3   Paperback: 122 pages

Learn to capture videos, manipulate images, and track objects with Python using the OpenCV Library

1. Set up OpenCV, its Python bindings, and optional Kinect drivers on Windows, Mac or, Ubuntu.

2. Create an application that tracks and manipulates faces.

3. Identify face regions using normal color images and depth images.

Please check **www.PacktPub.com** for information on our titles

16970719R00123

Made in the USA
Middletown, DE
05 January 2015